OKLAVA

OKLAVA

RECIPES FROM A
TURKISH-CYPRIOT KITCHEN

SELIN KIAZIM

This book is dedicated to my *Nene* (Grandma) Bahire,
for creating so much of my inspiration and forever pleasing
others through your incredible cooking and loving heart.

An Hachette UK Company
www.hachette.co.uk

First published in Great Britain
in 2017 by Mitchell Beazley,
a division of Octopus Publishing
Group Ltd, Carmelite House,
50 Victoria Embankment
London EC4Y 0DZ
www.octopusbooks.co.uk

ISBN 978 1 78472 246 3

A CIP catalogue record for this book is available from the British Library.
Printed and bound in China

10 9 8 7 6 5 4 3 2 1

Publishing Director: Stephanie Jackson
Art Director: Yasia Williams-Leedham
Design: Grade Design
Senior Editor: Alex Stetter
Photography: Chris Terry
Props Stylist: Cynthia Inions
Senior Production Manager: Peter Hunt

Ovens should be preheated to the specific temperature – if using a fan-assisted oven,
follow manufacturer's instructions for adjusting the time and the temperature.

CONTENTS

SELIN:
FROM THE BEGINNING

Oklava translates simply as 'rolling pin'. When I think of an *oklava* it always conjures up memories of my *nene* (grandmother): a rolling pin was never far from her hands, which always meant a delicious treat was imminent.

I was born and grew up in north London, surrounded by Turkish and Greek Cypriots. As all migrant communities seem to do, they'd all settled in one corner of London. As a result, Turkish grocers were always nearby, which made it very easy for Mum to bring us up on traditional Turkish fare, including dolmas, *yahni yemek*, *köfte*, *böreks* and, of course, kebabs.

My parents came over to London from Cyprus in the 1970s, but our ties to the country have always remained strong. My grandparents and cousins are all there, and our family has lived on the island for generations.

Thanks to its strategic location in the eastern Mediterranean, Cyprus has been ruled by many nations and settled by many cultures over the centuries. It has had Greek settlers for thousands of years, and in the early 1500s Turkish settlers (including my ancestors) arrived with the Ottoman Empire. Cyprus, as we now know it, has been peacefully divided in two since 1974, with the Turks living in the north and the Greeks in the south.

There is a huge amount of crossover between Turkish and Greek food. Much of it is practically the same, just with different names: for example, what is *şeftali* to us is *şeftalia* to the Greeks, and *köfte* is *keftedes*. The biggest difference between the two sides is that the Turks are Muslims and therefore do not eat pork, but the recipes are often essentially the same – one version will use lamb and the other pork.

The food of Cyprus is all about island cooking; it's simply what is grown on the land. Of course there are more supermarkets these days and some imports through Turkey, but shopping at the local market or even buying fruit and veg from roadside stalls is still very much how things are done, and in the villages they eat what they grow. Food in Cyprus is immensely seasonal, as I was reminded when looking for cauliflowers in June, while on a photo shoot for this book – there weren't any! And at certain times of the year, the dishes prepared in all the households will be similar. On that trip in June, a lot of the older women, including my grandmother, had black-stained hands from preparing *ceviz macunu*, candied walnuts. Making these is hugely laborious and takes a week. My grandmother doesn't even particularly like candied walnuts; she just makes them for the enjoyment of others!

In comparison to Turkish food with its Middle-Eastern influences, Cypriot cooking is very simple and more Mediterranean. In Turkey, with its history in the spice trade and influences from the Ottoman Empire, they use a lot more spices, as well as more nuts and dried fruits, to produce the most wonderful aromatic dishes, which can be quite rich. Cypriot flavours are simpler, ingredients lists shorter. There are also regional differences, with some areas of Turkey using butter as their main cooking fat and others olive oil.

First steps

In all honesty, I was pretty over Turkish food by the time I turned 19, which is when I enrolled at Westminster Kingsway College to study for a Professional Chef's Diploma. At college I learnt the basics of French cookery, which couldn't have been any further from Mum's cooking. I loved my years at college – it was the first time I felt like I was actually good at something. I was certainly never one for academic studies, but I did naturally lean towards the more creative subjects and had always loved to eat, so I guess it was perhaps inevitable that I would end up a chef.

Opposite: *In Cyprus with my grandfather, Kazım Doğramacı, my mother, Pervin Kiazim, and my grandmother, Bahire Doğramacı.*

I started at college thinking I would learn the basics and then perhaps work as a caterer, as I was pretty petrified by the idea of being a chef in a restaurant kitchen in London. Any thoughts of being a caterer quickly disappeared when I found myself completely at home in the college kitchens and immersed in cookery books. It became an obsession, and still is. I approached one of my college lecturers, Vince Cottam, who went on to mentor me through many competitions, including one that was run by the 'godfather of fusion' himself, New Zealand-born chef Peter Gordon. Competition day came, and that was the first time I met Peter. I was in my third and final year at college, and until then I had mostly met fairly intimidating head chefs on work experience. Now I was at the point where I needed to decide what kind of kitchen I wanted to work in. Peter was – and still is – the friendliest chef I have ever come across, and I knew I wanted to work for him

I won the competition and my prize was a five-week trip to New Zealand to work at some of the country's top restaurants. One of them was Dine by Peter Gordon, in a five-star hotel in Auckland. It was during my time there that Peter offered me the opportunity of a trial at his London restaurant, The Providores. I still clearly remember walking down the stairs to the kitchen for the first time, with Peter singing to me at the top of his voice. I worked a double shift that day and loved every minute of it: everyone in the kitchen was so friendly and made sure I tried as many different flavours as possible. No-one shouting? No angry head chef? My mind was blown from day one.

Moving on.
I couldn't have dreamt of a better start to my career: I learnt such an incredible amount at The Providores, not only about food, but also about how to interact with fellow team members and create a place where people genuinely wanted to work. Leaving was tough, but I knew I wanted my own restaurant some day, so I had to keep pushing myself and

climbing the ladder. There were no senior positions available at The Providores, so after two years I handed in my notice to Peter, crying my eyes out.

The job I had lined up didn't work out, and three months later I found myself working for Peter again, this time at his Covent Garden restaurant, Kopapa (now closed). After working at Kopapa as a sous chef for a year, I was made head chef. I was pretty confident in my cooking abilities at this point, but had never managed people before, so I found it a tough place to work. Again I learnt a lot, mostly about myself and my management style. Kopapa gave me a great insight into what it would take to open a new restaurant and how hard it is to make one successful.

By the end of 2012, my head was bursting with ideas and all I could think about was opening my own restaurant. I decided it was time to move on and try to make a name for myself. Pop-ups had become a big thing in London, so it seemed the natural platform for me to try it out. But before I could launch myself into the cut-throat London food scene, I had to decide what kind of food I wanted to present. I grew up in London, where the culture and the food are so diverse: it is incredibly inspiring to see people from all around the world take the humble cooking from their own countries and modernize it to work in London. The combination of my classical training at college, my Turkish-Cypriot family (including the time spent with my *nene* in her home village), my north London upbringing and four years exploring food from around the world with Peter Gordon gave me a great grounding that meant I could bounce off in any direction I wanted, but I hadn't ever really cooked my 'own' menu before.

Finding my own way
There were two things that led me to develop my style of modern Turkish cooking. First of all, there's nothing I love to eat more than a well-made kebab: anything cooked

over charcoal just tastes better! Second, I wanted to do something that no one else was doing, which is pretty much impossible, as there's always someone who thought of an idea before you – but that wouldn't stop me trying. I thought to myself, if I want to find something that sets me apart, I need to look at all the elements that make me the chef I am.

Once I finished working at Kopapa, I booked a trip to Istanbul and went in search of inspiration. I was already starting to lean towards more Middle-Eastern flavours in my cooking, and it occurred to me that all anyone thinks of when it comes to Turkish food are kebabs. Turkish food is rich, diverse and steeped in tradition, but relatively unexplored in the modern cooking world, and that was incredibly exciting for me. Even now, as I write this, we are exploring something new: earlier I was talking to my sous chef Nick about today's market special, a prawn köfte flatbread with smoked aubergine salad. I told him to mix some lamb suet into the fish köfte mixture and he thought I was slightly mad.

Opening the doors at Oklava

I got lucky while I was doing the pop-ups: after only a short while I was put in touch with the owners of what would become Trip Kitchen and Bar in Haggerston, east London. I spent a six-month residency there and was able to start showcasing the sort of food I wanted to cook. It went very well, but still not enough people knew about what I was doing. Then, one random evening towards the end of my time there, Giles Coren, the food critic for *The Times*, came in for dinner. To say I was petrified is a slight understatement; I immediately started doubting every dish on the menu, thinking he was going to hate everything and completely annihilate me. Somehow I managed to calm down, remember the faith I had in all my dishes and just cook to the best of my ability. It paid off, because he gave my food a glowing – if not perfect – review. I was gobsmacked. The review meant that I could leave Trip Kitchen on a massive high, with

the confidence of knowing that if I could just get to the point of opening my own place, I would certainly be in a position to compete with other London restaurants.

In the end it took just over 18 months to open the doors at Oklava. There were many opportunities along the way but nothing quite worked out, which made this phase of my life an incredibly frustrating time. I kept myself going with the occasional pop-up or event while searching for a site, funding and the right business partner. One of those events was a guest chef appearance at Salt Yard Group's Ember Yard in Soho. I didn't know it at the time, or even meet her then, but their operations manager, Laura Christie, would eventually become my business partner.

A few months passed before Laura and I met up to discuss the possibility of starting a restaurant together. This may sound like a cliché, but I knew immediately that Laura was just the person I was looking to partner up with. She is passionate about the industry, knowledgeable about service and wine, and great at all the things I'm not good at – and she loves a good Excel spreadsheet. I knew I wanted the restaurant to explore Turkish wines, and Laura not only expressed an interest in Middle-Eastern wines, but also, like me, wanted to do something with a wine list that no one else was doing. From that point on, we developed Oklava into what it is now.

This book brings together recipes that reflect my cooking style, inspired by my grandmother and mother. Some are a little complex – these are the Oklava dishes – but you will also find my versions of simple, traditional family recipes. I hope you will enjoy cooking from this book, or even using it as inspiration for your own dishes. Please don't just look at the pictures – I want to see grubby pages because you have been using this book so much!

LAURA:
MAKING IT WORK

When I first met Selin during my time at Salt Yard Group, I immediately knew she was someone I wanted to work with. As well as being fantastically talented, she had a clear vision of what she wanted to achieve and shared a lot of my own passions – not just the amazing produce and wine we are lucky enough to work with at Oklava, but also a real love of the restaurant industry. Knowing at that point very little about Turkish food, wine or culture, but realizing this was a special opportunity, I was quick to express my interest and we have been working together ever since.

From the beginning, we both felt it made sense to have a Turkish drinks list for a Turkish restaurant, and we set about researching what was available in the UK. With the help of friend and colleague Melisa Atay, herself the daughter of Turkish wine producers, we were introduced to some wineries and packed ourselves off to Istanbul to meet them.

This was my first time in Turkey and I had mixed feelings about our plan, having told everyone we were putting together an exclusively Turkish wine list and receiving some pretty shocked feedback. On arriving in Istanbul I was amazed to see that almost every restaurant's wine list was dominated not by Old World or even international producers, but by home-grown Turkish wineries. For those who have not had the pleasure of discovering Istanbul's dining scene, we are talking about some seriously impressive restaurants. We were lucky enough to meet some of the producers we now proudly list on our menu: Diren, Arcadia, Büyülübag and Paşaeli, to name a few. The passion, innovation and attention to detail shown by all of these wineries are second to none. It was an inspirational trip, and cemented our belief that Oklava was the perfect platform for modern Turkish wine. It suited our 'bring Turkish food to the London foodie' concept to a tee.

Keen to make sure this wasn't purely a rose-tinted vision (or perhaps a rosé-tinted one), we organized

a tasting back in the UK and were pleased to discover we had some diverse and delicious options for our list. Turkey is one of the oldest wine-growing areas in the world and has some brilliant producers, but, rather boringly, a combination of administrative red tape and very healthy demand at home keeps a lot of this wine from the international market, so we are delighted to be bringing a slice of it to London.

Alongside the wines we serve a small selection of cocktails, as well as Turkish classics – *rakı, çay* and Turkish coffee – recipes and serving suggestions for which you will find in the drinks chapter.

Although our recipes will, of course, work with more international pairings, serving the Oklava brunch with a Turkish Bloody Mary, surprising your guests with wine from a region they may never have tried before, or rounding off a delicious meal with a cup of Turkish coffee adds a special touch and really brings the Oklava experience to your home.

TOMATO, RAW ONION, PURSLANE, CRISP BREAD & MINT SALAD

SERVES 2–4

400g (14oz) stale bread, torn into 3cm (¹/₈in) chunks (old Baharat bread would be perfect; see page 46)

8 tablespoons best-quality extra-virgin olive oil

200g (7oz) tomatoes, best you can find, in different shapes and sizes

1 onion, thinly sliced

1 large bunch of purslane, leaves whole and stalks thinly sliced

4 long green Turkish peppers (Charleston peppers; use ordinary peppers if you can't find them), sliced

1 large handful mint leaves, shredded

1 handful flat leaf parsley

2 tablespoons red wine vinegar, or any good-quality vinegar

flaky sea salt and freshly ground black pepper

This salad is a version of one my *nene* makes. Hers is just a salad of yummy things from her garden, dressed with homemade olive oil and Turkish red wine vinegar. I very fondly remember eating this alongside the little fried fish she used to make; I would soak up the juices from the salad bowl with her freshly baked bread. Here I have combined all of that by putting the crisp bread into the salad to soak up the juices. This salad is great served alongside the Fried Red Mullet, Pickled Apricots & Caper Leaves (see page 123).

Preheat the oven to 170°C (325°F), Gas Mark 3. Put the stale bread on a baking tray and coat with 2 tablespoons of the olive oil and a little salt. Bake for about 15 minutes, or until crisp, checking it occasionally.

———

Cut the tomatoes into bite-sized pieces and place in a large bowl with the onion, purslane, peppers, mint and parsley. Once the crisp bread has cooled, add that too.

———

Season with salt and pepper and add the remaining olive oil and the vinegar. You can adjust the oil and vinegar quantities depending on how much dressing you like.

TOMATO-POMEGRANATE SALAD WITH PARSLEY

This is a version of *gavurdağ salatasi*, a famous salad from Turkey that also includes walnuts. It's inspired by a restaurant in Istanbul called Zubeyir, which turns out some of the best kebabs known to man. On my first visit I was encouraged by the waiter to order this salad, so I did – and it was utterly delicious. It's important to chop the vegetables very small so that they mingle with one another, but they don't have to be perfect dice. This salad is fantastic served with fatty meats.

Mix all the ingredients together in a large bowl and season with salt. It is best to let the salad sit for 5 minutes before serving. If you prefer, you can add more pomegranate molasses, depending on how acidic you like it.

SERVES 2–4

3 plum tomatoes, finely chopped

2 long green Turkish peppers (Charleston peppers; use ordinary peppers if you can't find them), finely chopped

1 large bunch of flat leaf parsley, finely chopped

1 red onion, finely chopped

50ml (2fl oz) pomegranate molasses

50ml (2fl oz) extra-virgin olive oil

flaky sea salt

ROMAINE LETTUCE SALAD WITH CANDIED WALNUTS & FETA DRESSING

I have been developing this recipe for quite a few years now. The idea initially came to me when I had an amazing salad at a fish restaurant called Uskumru in Istanbul. A bowl full of wonderful greens came to the table with a cheesy dressing. I couldn't work out quite what was in it, so in my very broken Turkish (some days I speak it better than others) I asked the waiter what was in it. The answer was 14 ingredients, and he wouldn't tell me any of them! This salad is pretty different from the one I got served that day. The best place to find candied walnuts is in a Turkish supermarket; they look like little black golf balls in syrup. They are candied when still in their green shells, fresh from the tree.

Start by making the dressing: place all the ingredients in a blender and process until smooth.

Slice the walnuts into 3mm (¹/₈in) slices. Lay all the lettuce leaves out on a tray with their cupped sides facing up. Spread the feta dressing inside all the leaves. Dot the walnut slices across the lettuce, then sprinkle over the chives. Finally, using a fine grater, grate the pecorino all across the top. Transfer to plates and serve.

SERVES 4

4 candied walnuts in syrup, or 100g (3½oz) walnuts, toasted

1 head of Romaine lettuce, separated into leaves

small bunch of chives, thinly sliced

30g (1oz) pecorino or hard sheeps' cheese

FOR THE DRESSING

300g (10½oz) Turkish white cheese or feta

1 garlic clove

1 teaspoon dried oregano

1 tablespoon honey

freshly squeezed juice of 1 lemon

100ml (3½fl oz) extra-virgin olive oil

80ml (2¾fl oz) water

SALAD OF RUNNER BEANS, CUCUMBER, FENNEL & KALE WITH A TOMATO DRESSING

1 fennel bulb

½ cucumber, cut into 5cm (2in) batons

50g (1¾oz) rocket

1 handful mint leaves, shredded

FOR THE KALE

250g (9oz) kale, central stalks sliced out and the leaves torn into small pieces

1 tablespoon extra-virgin olive oil

FOR THE BEANS

150ml (5fl oz) extra-virgin olive oil

1 onion, thinly sliced

4 garlic cloves, thinly sliced

1 teaspoon tomato purée

250g (9oz) runner beans, trimmed and sliced diagonally into 5mm (¼in) strips

4 tomatoes, coarsely grated

2 tablespoons sherry vinegar

flaky sea salt and freshly ground black pepper

The Turks love all sorts of beans, fresh or dried. Generally, they are cooked or dressed in lots of olive oil and tomato and served either as a vegetarian dish or cooked with lamb. Here I have made the dish into more of a salad, which is great for lunch or a light dinner. Find the best-quality runner beans you can in season – when they're at their best they have an incredible sweet flavour.

First prepare the beans. Preheat the oven to 130°C (250°F), Gas Mark 1. In a large, wide saucepan, heat the olive oil over a medium heat. Add the onion and stir to coat in the oil. Cover and cook gently for 5–10 minutes, stirring occasionally, until the onions are soft and translucent.

Add the garlic and tomato purée and cook for another 5 minutes. Stir in the runner beans, then cover and cook for another 10 minutes. Now add the tomatoes and season with salt and pepper. Cover and turn the heat right down. Cook for about 30 minutes, stirring occasionally, until the beans are completely soft and tender.

Meanwhile, coat the kale leaves in 1 tablespoon olive oil and a little salt. Spread them out flat on a baking tray and bake for about 15 minutes, or until crispy. Check the kale every 5 minutes and move it around on the tray so that it bakes evenly.

Check the beans: there should be just enough sauce to coat them. If there is too much, remove the lid and cook to reduce it. Turn the heat off and add the sherry vinegar. Taste and season with salt and pepper as needed. Allow to cool to room temperature before serving.

Cut the fennel into quarters lengthways through the root. Discard the dark green parts and cut out the core. Using a mandoline, slice the fennel quarters as paper thin as you can and place them in ice-cold water for 10 minutes. Alternatively, do this with a knife, but take your time to slice it as thinly as possible. Drain the fennel and dry it.

To assemble the salad, put the beans with all the tomato dressing in a large bowl, add the cucumber, fennel, rocket and mint and season with salt and pepper. Give it all a really good mix. Transfer to a serving dish, scatter with the kale crisps and serve immediately.

FRIED VEGETABLES WITH GARLIC YOGURT & POMEGRANATE

SERVES 4

2 courgettes, cut lengthways into 2cm (¾in) slices

2 aubergines, cut lengthways into 1cm (½in) slices

1 teaspoon fine salt

200–300ml (7–10fl oz) extra-virgin olive oil

8 long green Turkish peppers (Charleston peppers; use ordinary peppers if you can't find them), halved lengthways

4 hot Turkish peppers (sivri biber; use any hot chillies if you can't find them), halved lengthways (optional)

2 tablespoons pomegranate molasses

seeds from 1 pomegranate

flaky sea salt and freshly ground black pepper

FOR THE DRESSING

200ml (7fl oz) Turkish or Greek yogurt

100ml (3½fl oz) extra-virgin olive oil

1–3 garlic cloves (as much as you like!), finely grated

1 handful mint leaves, shredded

1 handful flat leaf parsley, shredded

Please note, you will be pretty garlicky after eating this! But you will also be licking your lips for more. Frying vegetables like this is pretty common in Turkey and Cyprus, especially during the summer. Find the best-tasting vegetables you can, as they are the stars of the show.

Sprinkle the courgettes and aubergines with the fine salt, put them in a colander, then set aside for 1 hour. This is to remove some of the excess moisture. Meanwhile, whisk together all the ingredients for the dressing with 3 tablespoons water and season with salt and pepper.

Rinse the salt off the courgettes and aubergines, then pat dry with kitchen paper.

In a large, shallow, wide-based pan, heat a quarter of the olive oil. Fry the courgettes, aubergines and peppers in batches until golden brown on both sides and cooked through, adding more olive oil as needed. As the vegetables cook, transfer them to a colander to cool and drain off the excess oil.

Once all the vegetables are at room temperature, coat them in the yogurt dressing and season with salt and pepper. Transfer to a serving dish, drizzle over the pomegranate molasses and scatter with the pomegranate seeds.

COURGETTE, FETA & MINT FRITTERS

In Turkey these fritters are known as *mücver*. Traditionally, they also include dill. Now, I know I have Turkish blood and all that, but I really don't like dill. That is why it's not in my recipe, but you can include it if you wish, along with any other herbs or greens you like. You could even try using different cheeses. I first put these on the menu at Trip Kitchen, and I can't say I really thought they would turn out to be as popular as they are, but everyone loves them and we get through loads of them every day. The secret is to add just enough flour so that they hold together when frying. The flour measurement below is not exact – it all depends on how much moisture is in your mixture. The fritters are best served with a little yogurt and extra shredded mint.

Mix the fine salt and courgettes together and put them in a colander set over a bowl. Sit a plate directly on top of the courgettes, then put several weights on top of the plate. Set aside for up to 1 hour to drain.

Put the courgettes in a clean tea towel and roll them up into a cracker shape, twisting the ends. Squeeze out as much liquid as you possibly can. Put them into a bowl and add the spring onions, mint, egg, cheese, flour and black pepper. Using your hands, mix together the whole lot, squeezing it as you go. It is important to combine the ingredients really well, but try to keep a little of the texture of the cheese.

Heat the sunflower oil in a deep-fat fryer to 180°C (350°F). Alternatively, place a deep frying pan over a high heat and add enough sunflower oil to cover the fritters. When hot enough, a small cube of bread added to the oil should sizzle immediately. Working in batches of 6–8, shape the fritter mixture into very tight quenelles using 2 identical spoons, and lower them into the oil one at a time. Fry for about 1–2 minutes, or until golden brown and crisp on each side. Remove and drain on kitchen paper. Repeat with the remaining mixture.

SERVES 4–6

1 teaspoon fine salt

8 courgettes, coarsely grated

2 bunches of spring onions, thinly sliced

1 large bunch of mint, leaves picked and shredded

1 large egg

800g (1lb 12oz) Turkish white cheese or feta, crumbled

200g (7oz) plain flour

freshly ground black pepper

sunflower oil, for frying

yogurt and shredded mint, to serve

FETA, GARLIC & POPPY SEED CRISPS

These are essentially fancy cheese crackers. But they're incredibly moreish, perfect as snacks or to serve alongside a cheese board. You could even top them with Muhammara (see page 190) and serve them as a canapé.

MAKES 18–24 CRISPS

200g (7oz) Turkish white cheese or feta, finely crumbled

40g (1½oz) poppy seeds or nigella seeds

2 garlic cloves, finely grated

40g (1½oz) unsalted butter, melted

4 sheets of filo pastry, each about 47 x 29cm (18 x 11in)

Preheat the oven to 200°C (400°F), Gas Mark 6. Line a large baking tray with baking parchment – the tray needs to be big enough to allow the filo sheets to sit completely flat.

———

Mix the feta, poppy seeds and grated garlic together. Brush the baking parchment with a little melted butter and lay a sheet of filo on top. Brush the top of the filo with more butter. Distribute one third of the feta mixture across the filo in a thin, even layer. Place another sheet of filo on top, pressing down firmly. Brush the top with butter.

———

Now distribute another third of the feta mixture across the filo in an even layer. Repeat the layering and brushing, finishing with a sheet of filo on top. Place a sheet of baking parchment on the filo and an identical baking tray on top of that. Push down firmly. Remove the top baking tray and paper and cut the filo sandwich into whatever shapes you wish. I like to cut rectangles.

———

Put the sheet of parchment back on top, followed by the baking tray. Bake for about 15 minutes, checking halfway through, or until golden brown and crisp. Remove the top baking tray and parchment and allow the crisps to cool completely.

CIRCASSIAN CHICKEN

SERVES 10–12 AS
PART OF A MEZE
SELECTION

1 whole free-range chicken
(about 1–1.3kg/2¼–3lb)

4 sprigs of thyme

1 head of garlic, cut in half
lengthways

2 tablespoons olive oil

1 onion, chopped

1 tablespoon chopped
rosemary

4 garlic cloves, finely grated

3 slices white bread, crusts
removed and cubed

500g (1lb 2oz) walnuts,
toasted and crushed

freshly squeezed juice
of 1–2 lemons

1–2 tablespoons sweet
smoked paprika

small bunch of flat leaf
parsley, finely chopped

small bunch of chives, thinly
sliced

fine salt

flaky sea salt and freshly
ground black pepper

While I was waiting for Oklava to open, I did a bit of private catering work. Whenever a customer wanted canapés, I made this recipe and served it on crostini, and it was a real winner. Called *çerkez tavuğu* in Turkish, this dish is also great as part of a meze spread.

Remove all the skin from the chicken and reserve it. Place the chicken, breast-side down in a large pan, along with the thyme and whole garlic, and just cover with water. Add a little fine salt. Bring to the boil over a high heat, then turn the heat right down to a gentle simmer. Cook for 45 minutes, turning the chicken over carefully after 30 minutes. Turn the heat off and leave the chicken in the liquid to cool completely.

Preheat the oven to 180°C (350°F fan), Gas Mark 4. Put the chicken skin on a baking tray and bake for 30 minutes, or until golden brown and crisp. Check it halfway through, at which point carefully drain off the excess fat and turn the skin over. Remove and drain on kitchen paper. Once cool, chop it finely.

Strain the stock off the chicken, reserving the liquid. Remove all the chicken meat from the bones and tear it into small pieces as you go.

Heat the olive oil in a small pan over a medium heat, add the onion and cook gently, without allowing them to colour, for 10 minutes. Add the rosemary and grated garlic and continue to cook for another 2 minutes. Remove and allow to cool slightly.

In a food processor, blend the onion mixture with the bread, half the walnuts, 500ml (18fl oz) of the reserved chicken cooking liquid, the juice of 1 lemon and 1 tablespoon paprika. Blend to a coarse purée.

Mix the purée with the chicken, the rest of the walnuts (reserving a few for garnish) and the parsley. Season with salt and pepper and add more lemon and paprika if you wish. Place on a serving dish and scatter over the chives, an extra sprinkling of paprika, a drizzle of olive oil, the reserved walnuts and the chicken skin.

OKLAVA BRUNCH

For as long I can remember, we always went on holiday to Cyprus or Turkey. There are big age gaps between my two older sisters and me – 7 and 15 years – and they stopped wanting to go on holiday with my parents as soon as they were old enough, but I still had to for many years ahead. Not that I'm complaining about being taken on holiday, but it became a lot less fun without my sisters there. However, there were two things that always got me excited: one was spending all day in the pool, the other was breakfast.

If we were staying in a hotel in Turkey, breakfast normally involved an array of breads, pastries, fresh and candied fruits, vegetables, yogurt, egg dishes, *Kayseri pastirma*, *sujuk* sausage, cheeses and much more. If we were in Cyprus, my *nene* would make me toast from bread she had baked during the week by grilling it over an open flame, then serve it with lashings of butter and her homemade strawberry jam, or sometimes her hellim (or halloumi, as this cheese is also known). I wish I could give you a recipe for her jam, but it would involve using the strawberries my grandparents grow. You will just have to take my word for it: it is the best strawberry jam in the world.

Breakfast or brunch, as I am about to explain, is not an everyday event; it's definitely a weekend thing. Midweek breakfast tends to involve just a few of the items listed opposite. At Oklava, we do our best to bring a little of that Turkish magic to the brunch we serve every weekend; we like people to take their time and work their way through the options.

BRUNCH MENU

HOUSE-BAKED BREADS
(SEE PAGES 46 & 52)

FETA, TULUM, KAŞAR
AND HELLIM CHEESES

MARINATED OLIVES

TAHINI WITH MULBERRY
MOLASSES

JAM

CANDIED FRUITS

CLOTTED CREAM

HONEY

SAVOURY AND SWEET
BÖREKS (SEE PAGES 55,
57, 58 & 204)

TOMATOES,
CUCUMBERS AND
TURKISH PEPPERS

SEASONAL FRUITS

KAYSERI PASTIRMA

MENEMEN
(SEE PAGE 40)

FRIED EGGS WITH
CYPRIOT PASTIRMA
(SEE PAGE 34)

MEDJOOL DATE BUTTER
(SEE PAGE 186)

ÇAY (SEE PAGE 166)

CYPRIOT PASTIRMA, BROKEN EGGS, SPICY TOMATO & BREAD SAUCE WITH TOMATO-POMEGRANATE SALSA & YOGURT

Mum would sometimes scramble eggs with *pastirma* as a quick dinner – so simple, yet so satisfying! It was the perfect treat. What we Cypriots call *pastirma* is called *sujuk* in mainland Turkey; although it comes in different forms, essentially it is cured beef flavoured with lots of garlic and paprika. You can find Cypriot *pastirma* or *sujuk* in most Turkish supermarkets, or you could use soft cooking chorizo or Merguez sausage instead.

Start by making the spicy tomato sauce. Heat the oil in a small saucepan, add the garlic, red chilli, chilli flakes and hot pepper paste and cook gently. Once completely soft, add the passata and water. Season with salt and pepper and simmer over a low heat for at least 30 minutes, stirring occasionally. If you can cook it for 1 hour, all the better, as it will intensify in flavour. Finish by adding the thyme, sugar and vinegar. Set aside and keep warm.

Combine all the ingredients for the salsa in a bowl and season with salt and pepper.

Slice each pastirma into about 6 pieces. Heat a large non-stick frying pan over a medium heat, add the pastirma and cook gently until nicely browned; there should be enough oil in the sausage, but if the pan seems a little dry, add a touch of olive oil. Crack in the eggs and use a spatula to scramble them into the pastirma. Season with a little salt. I like to cook the eggs so they are still soft, but you can cook them to your liking.

To assemble, stir the diced bread into the sauce and divide it between 4 bowls. Spoon the pastirma and eggs on top. Finish by putting a big spoonful of salsa in each bowl (making sure you get plenty of the juices), a dollop of yogurt, a final sprinkling of chilli flakes and some parsley to garnish. I like to serve this with toasted Turkish bread on the side and lashings of butter.

SERVES 4

- 400g (14oz) Cypriot pastirma (cured beef) slices
- 8 large eggs
- 200g (7oz) Turkish bread or a good white crusty loaf, diced into small pieces
- 4 tablespoons Turkish or Greek yogurt
- 1 tablespoon Turkish chilli flakes (pul biber)
- flat leaf parsley, chopped, to garnish

FOR THE SPICY TOMATO SAUCE

- 100ml (3½oz) extra-virgin olive oil
- 4 garlic cloves, sliced
- 1 red chilli, sliced, seeds left in
- 1 teaspoon Turkish chilli flakes (pul biber)
- 1 teaspoon Turkish hot pepper paste (açi biber salçasi)
- 500ml (18fl oz) tomato passata
- 100ml (3½fl oz) water
- 1 teaspoon thyme leaves
- 1 teaspoon caster sugar
- 2 teaspoons sherry or red wine vinegar
- flaky sea salt and freshly ground black pepper

FOR THE TOMATO-POMEGRANATE SALSA

- 2 tomatoes, diced
- small bunch of flat leaf parsley, shredded
- 2 tablespoons pomegranate molasses
- 4 tablespoons extra-virgin olive oil

SMOKED STREAKY BACON & MEDJOOL DATE BUTTER TOASTED SANDWICH

SERVES 2

8 rashers smoked streaky bacon

4 slices white crusty bread or sourdough

4 tablespoons Medjool Date Butter (see page 186)

2 tablespoons unsalted butter, at room temperature

In my opinion, this sandwich at the very least equals a good old-fashioned British bacon sandwich, if not tops it.

Cook the bacon to your liking in a frying pan or under the grill. Spread all 4 slices of bread with the date butter. Divide the bacon between 2 slices and top with the remaining 2 slices, butter side down. Spread the ordinary butter on the outside of both sandwiches.

———

Cook them in a toasted sandwich maker until golden and crisp. Alternatively, heat a frying pan over a medium heat, add the sandwiches, cover with a piece of baking parchment and place a weight on top (this ensures a lovely even colour). Cook until golden brown, then serve.

BROWN SHRIMP KAYGANA WITH PRESERVED LEMON HOLLANDAISE, ÇEMEN CRUMBS, CHIVES & SHEEP'S CHEESE

SERVES 4

sunflower oil, for cooking

100g (3½oz) peeled brown shrimps

small bunch of chives, sliced

100g (3½oz) hard sheep's cheese (such as pecorino), finely grated

flaky sea salt and freshly ground black pepper

FOR THE ÇEMEN CRUMBS

125g (4½oz) unsalted butter

1 tablespoon Çemen (see page 199)

250g (9oz) dried (preferably panko) breadcrumbs

FOR THE BATTER

2 tablespoons plain flour

6 large eggs

2 tablespoons milk

FOR THE PRESERVED LEMON HOLLANDAISE

1 small preserved lemon (see page 201)

250g (9oz) unsalted butter

1 large egg, plus 2 large egg yolks

freshly squeezed juice of ½ lemon

fine salt

A *kaygana* is essentially a cross between an omelette and a crêpe. You could add some herbs and spring onions to the batter and make a stack of them, or create sweet ones with nuts and syrup. But do try this recipe; I think it's a perfect marriage of flavours. Serve it with a big pile of toasted Turkish bread and plenty of butter.

Preheat the oven to 190°C (375°F), Gas Mark 5 and line a baking tray with baking parchment. First make the çemen crumbs: melt the butter with the çemen. Whisk well and stir in the breadcrumbs, ensuring they all get an even coating of butter and çemen; they should turn orange. Spread over the prepared tray. Bake for about 15 minutes, stirring them halfway through. Remove and leave to cool. Turn the oven down to 110°C (225°F), Gas Mark ¼.

———

For the batter, put the flour in a bowl and make a well in the centre. In a separate bowl, whisk the eggs and milk together. Add to the flour a little at a time, whisking continuously to form a smooth batter.

———

To make the hollandaise, cut the preserved lemon into quarters. Remove the flesh and squeeze the juice into a heatproof bowl. Dice the skin as finely as you can and set aside. Melt the butter in a pan and set aside to cool slightly. Whisk the egg and egg yolks into the lemon juice. Set the bowl over a pan of barely simmering water and whisk until the mixture leaves a trail that holds its shape when the whisk is lifted. Remove from the heat immediately and keep whisking until the eggs have cooled slightly.

———

Put the bowl on a tea towel or non-slip mat on the work surface. Whisking continuously with one hand, slowly pour in the melted butter with the other. If your hands get tired, pour in the butter a little at a time and whisk it all in before adding more. Once all the butter is incorporated, add the lemon juice and diced preserved lemon skin. Season with a little fine salt. Place a piece of clingfilm or parchment directly on top to stop a skin from forming.

———

Heat 1 tablespoon oil over a medium heat in a frying pan about 20cm (8in) in diameter. Scatter a quarter of the shrimps around the pan, then pour in a quarter of the batter and season with salt and pepper. Cook until the top is lightly golden and the underside is set. Fold in half to make a semicircle and continue to cook for about 20 seconds, then flip it over and cook for another 20 seconds, until both sides are golden. Transfer to a baking tray and keep warm. Repeat this step to make 3 more. Put them all in the oven to warm up for 2–3 minutes.

———

To serve, put one kaygana in the centre of each serving plate, drizzle over some hollandaise and scatter over the chives, çemen crumbs and grated cheese.

MENEMEN

I make my *menemen* a little differently from most recipes, although everyone has their own version – you can even add feta, *sujuk* or *Kayseri pastirma*, if you like. Traditionally, you would just sauté the vegetables quite quickly and then scramble the eggs in; if you find good enough produce, you can make it just like that. I prefer to make a ragout first and get the best I can out of all the flavours. You can make the ragout ahead of time and chill it in the fridge. To cook the dish, simply pour more olive oil into a frying pan, add the ragout to heat up gently, then crack in the eggs and cook as described. Long green Turkish peppers (known as Charleston peppers) and hot green sivri peppers are distinctive flavours in Turkish cooking, and are available in most Turkish supermarkets. If you can't get hold of them, just use ordinary green peppers and green chillies respectively.

Heat the oil in a large frying pan, add the onion and peppers and cook gently over a low heat for about 30 minutes, or until completely soft. Add the tomato purée, hot pepper paste and tomatoes and cook gently for another 30 minutes. Season with a little salt and pepper at this point. Finish the sauce base by adding the sugar and vinegar.

———

Crack the eggs into the pan and, using a spatula, gently cook them, stirring, to a soft scrambled consistency. Season with salt and pepper and then garnish with parsley. Serve with lots of freshly baked bread.

SERVES 4

- 150ml (5fl oz) extra-virgin olive oil
- 1 onion, diced
- 4 long green Turkish peppers (Charleston peppers; use ordinary peppers if you can't find them), sliced
- 4 hot Turkish peppers (sivri biber; use any hot chillies if you can't find them), sliced
- ½ teaspoon tomato purée
- 1 teaspoon Turkish hot pepper paste (açi biber salçasi)
- 4 plum tomatoes, roughly blitzed in a food processor or grated
- ½ teaspoon caster sugar
- ½ teaspoon sherry or red wine vinegar
- 8 large eggs
- flat leaf parsley, chopped, to garnish
- flaky sea salt and freshly ground black pepper

PISTACHIO-CRUSTED BANANA & TAHINI FRENCH TOAST WITH ORANGE BLOSSOM SYRUP & SMOKED STREAKY BACON

I first came across stuffed French toast when I started working at The Providores. The restaurant's famous version is stuffed with banana and pecans and served with bacon and verjus syrup. I created this version one day when I needed to use up a pile of small baguettes that had gone stale, so feel free to try it with a baguette too – it will just need longer soaking.

Preheat the oven to 190°C (375°F), Gas Mark 5. Whisk the eggs and double cream together in a shallow bowl and set aside. Put the pistachios on a baking tray and and bake for about 6 minutes, or until lightly toasted and smelling nutty. Leave them to cool, then crush to a coarse powder in a food processor or with a pestle and mortar and spread them out on a plate.

———

Peel and roughly crush the bananas in a bowl. Using a spatula, mix the tahini and mascarpone together in a separate bowl, then mix it through the bananas. Spread this mixture over 2 slices of bread. Top with the remaining slices and press down gently to stick the whole sandwich together.

———

Dip the sandwiches in the egg and cream mixture, turning to coat well, then leave them to soak up the mixture for 10 minutes, turning halfway through to make sure both sides get soaked.

———

Set a large frying pan over a medium heat and add the oil and butter. Once the butter has melted, add the sandwiches and cook for about 5 minutes on each side until golden brown.

———

Meanwhile, in another frying pan or under the grill, cook the bacon to your liking (for me it has to be crispy!).

———

Remove the sandwiches from the pan and put them on a baking tray. Brush each side with some orange blossom syrup, then dip them straight into the pistachio crumbs, coating well on both sides. Cut in half and serve topped with the bacon and more syrup.

SERVES 2

2 large eggs

200ml (7fl oz) double cream

150g (5½oz) peeled pistachios

1 large or 2 small bananas

2 tablespoons tahini

3 heaped tablespoons mascarpone

4 slices white crusty bread

1 tablespoon sunflower oil

2 heaped tablespoons unsalted butter

6 rashers smoked streaky bacon

½ quantity Orange Blossom Syrup (see page 200)

SAVOURY
BAKES

BAHARAT-SPICED BREAD

This recipe is adapted slightly from the village bread my *nene* makes. I have fond memories of eating it fresh from the clay oven with lashings of butter. She perfumes the bread with just a little *baharat*, which she mixes in after the dough has proved once so that it ripples throughout the bread. *Baharat* is a blend of spices that usually includes allspice, cloves, cinnamon and nutmeg, although everyone has their own recipe which sometimes includes other spices. My *nene* would also break some of the bread into chunks as soon as it was baked, then dry them out in the residual heat of the oven. This is known as *peksimet*, or dried bread, and is usually doused in water just before serving.

If using fresh yeast, dissolve it in about 150ml (5fl oz) lukewarm water with the sugar.

If using dried yeast, mix it with the flour, sugar and salt in a large bowl. Make a well in the centre and add the olive oil, baharat and 150ml (5fl oz) lukewarm water. If using fresh yeast, mix the flour and salt in a large bowl, make a well in the centre and add the frothy yeast mixture along with the olive oil and baharat.

Using your hands, begin to incorporate the flour into the liquid. Slowly add more lukewarm water a little at a time, mixing with your hands to form a dough. (You'll probably need around another 150ml (5fl oz), but don't add it all at once; you'll only need extra if it feels dry). Tip the dough onto a lightly floured surface. Knead for about 5 minutes, or until smooth.

Put the dough in a clean bowl and cover it with a clean, damp tea towel. Place somewhere slightly warm to speed up the rising process; the dough should double in size, within 45–60 minutes.

Preheat the oven to 240°C (475°F), Gas Mark 9. Punch the dough down in the bowl, then tip it onto a very lightly floured surface. Knead the dough for around 30 seconds. Roll the bread into a cylinder about 8cm (3¼in) in diameter. Cut it into 3 equal pieces, then push them together lightly. Place the sesame seeds on a large plate. Brush the dough all over with a little water and press it lightly into the sesame seeds, turning so it is covered on all sides. Place on a lightly floured nonstick baking tray and set aside to prove. It should double in size within about 45 minutes.

Half-fill a glass with cold water. Put the dough in the oven, tip the water directly onto the bottom of your oven and immediately close the door. Bake for 20 minutes, then lower the heat to 200°C (400°F), Gas Mark 6 and continue to bake for another 10–20 minutes, or until golden brown. To check if it is cooked, tap on the bottom and listen for a hollow sound. If it doesn't sound hollow, return it to the oven for a little longer. Remove and leave to cool down considerably before cutting it.

MAKES 1 LOAF

15g (½oz) fresh yeast or
  1 x 7g sachet fast-action
  dried yeast
½ teaspoon caster sugar
450g (1lb) strong bread flour
1 teaspoon fine salt
1 teaspoon olive oil
1 tablespoon baharat (see
  page 193; also available in
  Turkish supermarkets)
3 tablespoons mixed white
  and black sesame seeds

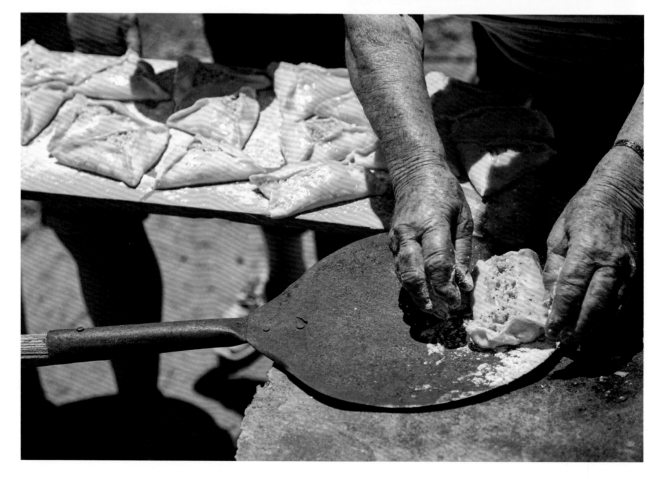

PILAVUNA

MAKES 12

about 750g (1lb 10oz) hellim cheese, finely grated

1 tablespoon dried mint

1 teaspoon baking powder

2 heaped tablespoons fine semolina

100g (3½oz) sultanas (optional)

4–6 large eggs

FOR THE DOUGH

750g (1lb 10oz) plain flour

1 teaspoon fine salt

1 x 7g sachet fast-action dried yeast

about 450ml (16fl oz) lukewarm water

1 teaspoon caster sugar

1 teaspoon olive oil

TO FINISH

100g (3½oz) sesame seeds, moistened with 1 tablespoon water (optional)

1–2 large eggs, lightly beaten

Pilavuna are very traditional Cypriot pastries, perfect as a teatime treat or for breakfast. My mum and her friends often gather of an evening to knock up a massive batch of these, along with other pastries. They have a coffee and gossip, and then each person takes home their share of baked goods.

First make the dough: put the flour in a large bowl and add the salt on one side and the yeast and the sugar on the other. Gradually add the water, incorporating the flour with your hands as you go. Once a dough has formed, turn it onto a clean work surface and knead until smooth. Clean any crumbs out of the bowl, grease it with the olive oil, then add the dough. Cover it with clingfilm or a damp cloth and leave to prove in a warm place until doubled in size (about 45 minutes).

———

Meanwhile, make the filling. Put the hellim in a bowl with the mint, baking powder, semolina and sultanas, if using and mix well. Work in the eggs one at a time until a dough forms. You might need a little extra semolina to achieve this. Divide the mixture into 12 equal pieces. Preheat the oven to 220°C (425°F), Gas Mark 7. Line 2–3 baking trays (depending on size) with baking parchment.

———

Turn the dough onto a lightly floured work surface and knead lightly for a minute or so. Roll it into a large sausage shape, then divide it into 12 equal pieces. Roll each piece of dough into a 10 x 8cm (4 x 3in) rectangle, about 3mm (⅛in) thick. Press one side of the dough into the moistened sesame seeds so that they stick to it. Return it to the work surface and place 1 portion of the filling in the centre. Fold up the edges of the dough to make a rectangular shape, leaving some of the filling exposed in the centre. Place on the baking sheet and repeat the process for the remaining filling and dough.

———

Brush the top of the pastries with beaten egg to glaze and sprinkle over a few extra sesame seeds if you wish. Bake for 20–25 minutes, or until golden brown all over.

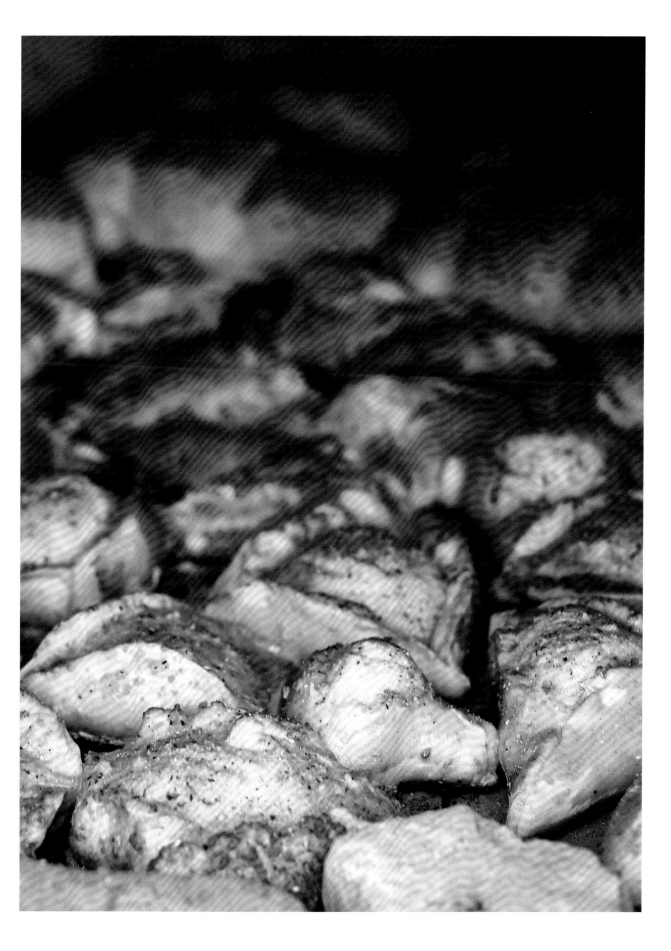

BLACK OLIVE, HELLIM, ONION & MINT LOAF

This is one of my favourites of my Mum's recipes. It features quite a bit of olive oil, which gives a lovely, almost focaccia-like texture – perfect with a cup of tea in the afternoon. Make sure you use the best olives you can find, as these are key to the flavour.

In a large bowl, mix together the flour, yeast, salt and sugar. Add the water and olive oil to form a thick batter. Add the remaining ingredients and mix well. Oil a roasting tin measuring about 36 x 26 x 5cm (14 x 10 x 2in) or a round baking tin about 30cm (12in) in diameter. Place the batter into the tin and even out. Leave to prove until doubled in size.

——

Preheat the oven to 210°C (400°F), Gas Mark 6. Bake for 45–60 minutes or until golden brown. Insert a skewer to check; if it comes out clean, the loaf is ready. Leave to cool.

SERVES 14–16

1kg (2lb 4oz) plain flour

2 x 7g sachets fast-action dried yeast

1 teaspoon fine salt

1 teaspoon caster sugar

800ml (1¹/₃ pints) water

1 onion, finely chopped

250g (9oz) hellim cheese, cut into 1cm (½in) dice

500g (1lb 2oz) good-quality pitted black olives, roughly chopped

250ml (9fl oz) extra-virgin olive oil, plus extra for greasing

2 tablespoons dried mint

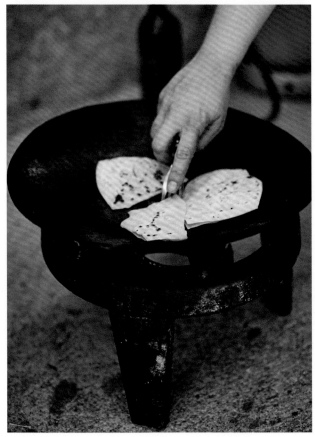

CHEESE, SPRING ONION, BAHARAT & GARLIC BÖREKS

MAKES 18-20

500g (1lb 2oz) mixed cheese, grated

1 bunch of spring onions, thinly sliced

large bunch of flat leaf parsley, finely shredded

2 tablespoons baharat (see page 193; also available in Turkish supermarkets)

4 garlic cloves, finely grated

1 quantity Pide dough (see page 60)

plain flour, for dusting

2 tablespoons extra virgin olive oil, for drizzling

These are perfect for an afternoon snack or even for breakfast, and the baharat gives a lovely background perfume. Feel free to use whatever kind of cheese you prefer, or even just one type. I like to use a mix of aged kaşar cheese, feta and hellim, but mature Cheddar, Parmesan and soft goats' cheese work well too.

Combine the cheeses, spring onions, parsley, baharat and garlic. Divide into 2 equal portions and set aside.

———

Once the pide dough has risen, punch it down and divide into 2 equal balls. Keep one covered and, on a lightly floured work surface, roll the other into a rough circle about 2mm ($^1/_{16}$in) thick. Place tablespoons of the cheese mixture on one half of the dough, ensuring each spoonful is at least 3cm (1¼in) from the next. Fold the other half of the dough over them and press it down quite firmly around the piles of filling.

———

Using either a pizza cutter or a small sharp knife, cut around the piles of filling to make random shapes. If the edges of each börek have not stuck together securely, use a little water to seal them. Place the böreks on a lightly floured surface. Repeat the process with the remaining dough and filling.

———

Heat a large, heavy-based frying pan on a medium-high heat. Place 4 or 5 böreks in the dry pan and cook for 2–3 minutes, turning regularly, or until dark brown spots appear. Repeat until all the böreks are cooked. Drizzle with olive oil to serve.

SPICED BEEF & CHEESE SAUCE POĞAÇAS

When in need of a top-up of Turkish ingredients, I often pop into my local TFC (Turkish Food Centre). These shops are scattered all around London and have their own in-house bakeries, which make the most incredible baked goods. I find it pretty hard to resist their *poğaças*, which are small, brioche-like buns that are often stuffed with feta and parsley. You can experiment with different types of filling, but don't put anything too wet inside or they might pop open.

Start by making the dough. Combine the flour, yeast, sugar and salt in a bowl. Make a well in the centre and add 2 eggs, the melted butter, yogurt and water. Bring together with your hands and knead for about 5 minutes on a lightly floured surface to form a smooth dough. Place in a clean bowl and cover with a clean damp tea towel. Set aside to rise for about 45 minutes, or until doubled in size.

———

Meanwhile, make the filling. Heat the oil in a large saucepan over a high heat. Add the mince and cook, using a whisk to break it up, until browned all over, stirring occasionally. This will take about 8 minutes. Add the onions and continue to cook over a medium heat until lightly browned. Now add the remaining ingredients (except the sesame seeds) and cook over a medium-low heat for about 20 minutes. Set aside to cool.

———

To make the cheese sauce, melt the butter in a medium saucepan. Add the flour, whisk well and cook over a low heat for 5 minutes. Add one-third of the milk and whisk it in until smooth. Repeat with the remaining milk. Continue to cook over a low heat, whisking occasionally, for 15 minutes. Finally, add both the cheeses and cook for another 2 minutes. Set aside and allow to cool.

———

Preheat the oven to 200°C (400°F), Gas Mark 6 and line a large baking tray with baking parchment. Punch down the dough and divide it into 12–14 equal pieces on a lightly floured surface. Roll a piece of dough into a circle about 12cm (5in) in diameter. Place a heaped tablespoon of cheese sauce in the centre and spread it out slightly, ensuring you leave a 2cm (¾in) border all the way around the edge. Do the same with the beef filling. Fold over the dough to make a pasty shape, ensuring you press down the edges to seal them well. Place it on the prepared baking tray. Repeat the with the remaining dough, leaving a 2cm (¾in) gap between each one (you might need more than one baking tray).

———

Beat the remaining egg with about 2 tablespoons water, brush the pastries with this mixture and sprinkle with sesame seeds. Bake for 16–18 minutes, or until golden brown.

MAKES 12

2 tablespoons sunflower oil

500g (1lb 2oz) minced beef

2 onions, finely chopped

large bunch of flat leaf parsley, finely chopped

2 tablespoons Turkish hot pepper paste (açi biber salçasi)

1 heaped tablespoon tomato purée

1 teaspoon ground cumin

1 teaspoon ground fennel

1 teaspoon sweet smoked paprika

1 teaspoon ground coriander

50g (1¾oz) mixed white and black sesame seeds

flaky sea salt and freshly ground black pepper

FOR THE DOUGH

700g (1lb 9oz) plain flour

10g (¼oz) fast-action dried yeast

40g (1½oz) caster sugar

¾ teaspoon fine salt

3 large eggs

165g (5¾oz) unsalted butter, melted

300ml (10fl oz) strained yogurt

100ml (3½fl oz) water

FOR THE SAUCE

100g (3½oz) unsalted butter

75g (2¾oz) plain flour

800ml (1¹/₃ pints) milk

80g (2¾oz) hard cheese, such as pecorino, grated

140g (5oz) hellim cheese, grated

BAHARAT & CHILLI-SPICED FISH BÖREKS

MAKES 10–12

1 egg white, for brushing
12 sheets of filo pastry
sunflower oil, for frying

FOR THE FILLING

100ml (3½fl oz) extra-virgin olive oil

1 large onion, diced

3 garlic cloves, finely grated

2 tablespoons sweet pepper paste (tatli biber salçasi)

1 tablespoon baharat (see page 193; also available in Turkish supermarkets)

2–4 tablespoons urfa chilli flakes (isot biber), depending on how hot you like it

2 teaspoons sweet smoked paprika

300g (10½oz) skinless fish fillet, diced

50g (1¾oz) sultanas

1 large handful mint leaves, shredded

1 large handful flat leaf parsley, shredded

flaky sea salt and freshly ground black pepper

These *böreks* would work well with all types of white fish, such as pollock, cod or haddock. You could even mix some prawns or crab in there too. I think they're great as party food, or if you want to be a little fancy, you could serve one of them alongside a piece of roasted fish for a dinner party.

Start by making the filling. Heat the oil in a large frying pan, add the onion and cook gently over a medium heat until golden brown. Add the garlic, sweet pepper paste, baharat, chilli flakes and paprika and continue to cook for 5 minutes. Add the fish and sultanas and cook for another 5 minutes, or until the fish is just cooked through. Remove from the heat and season with salt and black pepper. Transfer to a tray and spread it out to cool down quickly. Once cool, mix in the herbs and divide the mixture into 12 equal portions.

—

Beat the egg white lightly in a small bowl, just to break it up. Place a sheet of filo on a work surface with the long side nearest you. Fold it in half from left to right. Now place one portion of the filling in the centre of the edge closest to you, leaving a 4cm (1½in) gap on each side. From the edge closest to you, fold the filo over the filling twice. Now fold in the sides. Brush the remaining pastry with egg white and continue to roll it up, ensuring you encase the filling tightly. Repeat this process with the remaining filo and filling.

—

Heat the oil in a deep-fat fryer to 180°C (350°F). Alternatively, place a deep frying pan over a high heat and add enough oil to cover the böreks. When hot enough, a small cube of bread added to the oil should sizzle immediately.

—

Carefully add 4 böreks to the oil and fry for 1–2 minutes, or until golden brown. You might need to turn them over halfway if they don't colour evenly. Remove and drain on kitchen paper, then fry the remaining böreks in the same way. Serve immediately.

SPINACH & FETA BÖREK

I'm not usually a huge fan of spinach, but in this *börek* I am. You can use other fillings too, such as a selection of cheeses, nuts, mushrooms and so on. Made as a large pie, rather than individual pastries, this is a favourite at Oklava as part of our brunch.

MAKES 1 X 30CM
(12IN) PIE
(8–12 SERVINGS)

100ml (3½fl oz) extra-virgin
olive oil

2 onions, finely chopped

1kg (2lb 4oz) large leaf
spinach with stalks,
roughly chopped (or
2 large bags of spinach
leaves, 450g/1lb each)

2 large eggs

200ml (7fl oz) double cream

800g (1lb 12oz) Turkish white
cheese or feta

1 tablespoon dried oregano

large bunch of flat leaf
parsley, finely chopped

24 sheets of filo pastry, about
48 x 25cm (19 x 10in) each

125g (4½oz) unsalted butter,
melted

flaky sea salt and freshly
ground black pepper

Heat 2 tablespoons of the oil in a small saucepan, add the onions and cook gently until golden brown. Place a large heavy-based pan over a high heat with one-third of the remaining olive oil. Add one-third of the spinach and cook until just wilted. Transfer to a colander set over a bowl and repeat the process with the rest of the spinach and oil in 2 batches. Squeeze out as much water from the spinach as possible, then combine it with the cooked onions and season with salt and pepper. Whisk together the eggs and cream.

―――

Preheat the oven to 210°C (400°F), Gas Mark 6. Crumble the cheese into a bowl and stir in the oregano and parsley. To assemble the börek, start by brushing a 30 x 20 x 4cm (12 x 8 x 1½in) baking tray or a 30cm (12in) round baking tin with butter. Lay a sheet of filo in the tray, allowing it to hang over the edges, brush the filo with butter, then add another sheet on top. Repeat the process with 4 more filo layers, making sure some pastry hangs over on all sides.

―――

Spread half the spinach mixture over the filo and pour in one-quarter of the egg mixture. Layer up another 4 sheets of filo, this time cutting each sheet in half so that the pastry does not hang over the edges, and brushing with butter in between each one. Now spread half the cheese mixture over the top and pour in one-quarter of the egg mixture. Top with another 4 halved sheets of filo, brushing each one with butter as before.

―――

Spread over the remaining spinach mixture and pour in one-quarter of the egg mixture. Top with another 4 halved sheets of filo, brushing them with butter as before. Now spread over the final layer of cheese mixture, pour in the remaining egg mixture and press the whole lot down evenly.

―――

Fold the overhanging edges of filo over the top. Finish the börek with 6 whole sheets of filo, brushing with butter in between each one and pushing in the edges with the handle of a metal spoon as you go. Brush the top with butter. Bake for 25 minutes, then turn the oven down to 190°C (375°C), Gas Mark 5 and bake for another 20 minutes. Allow the börek to cool before cutting it into 12 portions.

PIDES

When designing Oklava, there were two features I just had to include. One is our barbecue and the other is our big stone oven, where we make our *pides* and *lahmacun*, Turkish versions of pizza. The heat is so intense that you get an amazing crust on breads and pastry products. Chances are you won't have a stone oven at home, but these *pides* work really well in a conventional oven too. *Lahmacuns* don't, however, which is why I haven't included a recipe here.

Traditionally, *pides* have toppings such as Turkish cheeses, peppers, onions, tomatoes, diced lamb or chicken. One of my favourites, which I always asked for when I was younger, has a little tomato sauce, Cypriot *pastirma* and an egg, and is delicious to eat hot or cold. As with everything we do at Oklava, these traditional *pides* are our source of inspiration for creating more contemporary versions. You could have a go at a simple version here before moving on to our more complex ones. For example, try mixing minced lamb with diced onions, peppers, tomato and parsley, then place the raw mixture on rolled-out pide dough and bake as below. Alternatively, you could try a mix of mozzarella, Cheddar, crumbly goats' cheese and chopped parsley.

PIDE DOUGH

If using fresh yeast, dissolve it in a little water. Place the flour, yeast, olive oil, salt and sugar in a large bowl or stand mixer. Mix well, then slowly begin to add the water, mixing with one hand. Do not add all the water at once, as you might not need it all. Add just enough to form a dough that doesn't stick to your hands too much.

———

Tip it onto a clean, lightly floured surface. Knead for 5 minutes, or until a smooth dough forms. Shape it into a ball, put it in a clean bowl and cover with a clean damp tea towel. Leave it somewhere warm for 45–60 minutes until doubled in size.

———

Once the dough has risen, punch it back in the bowl, then tip onto a lightly floured surface. Roll the dough into a

long sausage, then divide it into 6 equal pieces. Roll each piece into a ball, put them on a lightly floured surface and cover with a damp tea towel until you're ready to use them.

———

Preheat the oven to 240°C (475°F), Gas Mark 9. Put a pizza stone or a large flat baking tray in the oven.

———

Place a ball of dough on a floured work surface and roll into an oval about 40 x 15cm (16 x 6in). Combine the raw ingredients of your chosen filling, place them on the rolled-out dough and fold in the edges as shown opposite. Slide onto a baking sheet. Make 5 more in the same way, then bake for 10–12 minutes.

MAKES 6

625g (1lb 6oz) strong white bread flour (we use a Turkish flour called Bodrum), plus extra for dusting

12g (¹/₃oz) fresh yeast or 1 x 7g sachet fast-action dried yeast

1 tablespoon extra-virgin olive oil

1 teaspoon fine salt

1 teaspoon caster sugar

340–360ml (11–13fl oz) lukewarm water

SIMPLE FILLING 1

500g (1lb 2oz) minced lamb

1 onion, diced

2 peppers, chopped

4 tomatoes, chopped

small bunch of parsley, chopped

SIMPLE FILLING 2

200g (7oz) Cheddar cheese, grated

200g (7oz) mozzarella cheese, diced

200g (7oz) goats' cheese, crumbled

small bunch of parsley, chopped

CHICKEN & GARLIC KÖFTE PIDE WITH CHILLI YOGHURT, SMOKED SALSA, WALNUTS & FETA

MAKES 6

1 quantity Pide dough (see page 60)

flour, for dusting

2 tablespoons unsalted butter, melted

½ quantity Fried Dried Chilli Yogurt (see page 199)

120g (4¼oz) walnuts, lightly toasted and crushed

120g (4¼oz) feta

small handful mint, finely shredded

small handful flat leaf parsley, finely shredded

FOR THE CHICKEN KÖFTE

500g (1lb 2oz) minced chicken

1 red pepper, finely diced

1 onion, finely diced

3 garlic cloves, finely grated

100g (3½oz) sweet pepper paste (tatlı biber salçası)

small bunch of flat leaf parsley, finely chopped

fine salt

FOR THE SALSA

6 banana shallots, skin on, halved lengthways

250g (9oz) baby plum tomatoes

10 long green Turkish peppers (Charleston peppers; use ordinary peppers if you can't find them)

2 tablespoons pomegranate molasses

1 teaspoon sweet smoked paprika

1 teaspoon dried oregano

100ml (3½fl oz) extra-virgin olive oil

flaky sea salt

Here is one of those recipes that just came to me, this time during a conversation with my sous chef, Nick. He was telling me that he missed cooking the lamb *köfte* we'd once had on the menu, while I was thinking that I wanted to put a new meat *pide* on. The result was that I combined them.

Preheat the oven to 240°C (475°F), Gas Mark 9. Put a pizza stone or a large flat baking tray in the oven.

———

Mix together all the ingredients for the chicken köfte. Season with salt, then fry a little and taste it: adjust the seasoning, as necessary and divide the mixture into 6 equal portions.

———

To make the smoked salsa, you'll need a hot barbecue or a very hot ridged griddle pan. Working in batches, cook the shallots, tomatoes and peppers until their skins are blackened. Allow them to become cool enough to handle, then peel off the shallot and pepper skins and dice the flesh. Peel and crush the tomatoes with the back of a fork and combine them in a bowl with the shallots and peppers and the remaining ingredients for the salsa. Season with salt.

———

Opposite: *Chicken & Garlic Köfte Pide with Chilli Yogurt, Smoked Salsa, Walnuts & Feta (top); Braised Octopus Pide with Ricotta, Green Olives, Honey, Pickled Caper Shoots & Thyme (centre) and Cheese Sauce Pide with Charred Leeks & Crispy Potatoes (bottom).*

To make the pides (I suggest making them one at a time), roll out a ball of dough on a floured surface into a large oval shape about 40 x 15cm (16 x 6in). Spread one portion of the chicken köfte mixture down the centre, leaving a border of 3cm (1¼in) around the edge. Season with a little flaky salt. Fold in the sides as shown on page 61, and pinch the ends together really well so that the pide doesn't unravel during baking.

———

Slide your pide onto a very flat baking sheet, then place it on the preheated baking tray or pizza stone. Bake for 10–12 minutes, or until golden brown and crisp on the outside. Remove and brush the sides of the pide with the melted butter, then top with some smoked salsa, chilli yogurt, walnuts, feta, mint and parsley. Make 5 more in the same way. If you want to serve the pides all together, set them aside after baking, then reheat and garnish as described.

BRAISED OCTOPUS PIDE WITH RICOTTA, GREEN OLIVES, HONEY, PICKLED CAPER SHOOTS & THYME

The flavours of this *pide* – my favourite – are quite unusual and I find that customers often love it because they aren't expecting it to work. If you're not a fan of sweet with savoury I suggest leaving out the honey. Use capers if you can't find pickled caper shoots (they are available in Turkish supermarkets) and substitute pre-marinated octopus if you can't source fresh.

Preheat the oven to 170°C (325°F), Gas Mark 3. Put the octopus in a large roasting tray along with half the olive oil and a lemon half. Cover with foil and bake for 1½–2 hours until tender. The best way to check if the octopus is ready is to cut a little off and taste it; if it is chewy, it needs a little longer. Remove and drain the octopus and allow it to cool completely.

If you happen to be having a barbecue, grill the octopus over hot coals until well coloured and a little charred on both sides. Alternatively, heat a ridged griddle pan until very hot and cook the octopus in the same way.

Preheat the oven to 240°C (475°F), Gas Mark 9. Put a pizza stone or a large flat baking tray in the oven. Cut off the octopus legs and cut them into 1cm (½in) slices. Remove the beak and any other tough bits in the centre, then rinse the head and cut it into 1cm (½in) slices.

Put the remaining olive oil in a bowl along with the rosemary, garlic and vinegar, and season with salt and

pepper. Leave the octopus to marinate in the refrigerator for as long as you can, preferably overnight.

To make the pides (I suggest making them one at a time), roll out a ball of dough on a floured surface into a large oval shape about 40 x 15cm (16 x 6in). Spread one-sixth of the ricotta down the middle, leaving a border of 3cm (1¼in) border around the edge. Sprinkle over some thyme and green olives and season with salt and pepper. Top with a layer of the octopus. Fold in the sides as shown on page 61, and pinch the ends together really well so that the pide doesn't unravel during baking.

Slide your pide onto a very flat baking sheet, then place it on the preheated baking tray or pizza stone. Bake for about 10–12 minutes, or until golden brown and crisp on the outside. Remove and brush the sides with the melted butter, then top with the caper shoots, a drizzle of honey and some ricotta shavings. Make 5 more in the same way. If you want to serve the pides all together, set them aside after baking, then reheat and garnish as described.

MAKES 6

- 1.5–2kg (3lb 5oz–4lb 8oz) octopus
- 150ml (5fl oz) extra-virgin olive oil
- 1 lemon, halved
- 2 sprigs of rosemary
- 3 garlic cloves, lightly crushed
- 3 tablespoons Turkish red wine vinegar, or any good-quality vinegar
- 1 quantity Pide dough (see page 60)
- flour, for dusting
- 6 heaped tablespoons ricotta cheese
- 3 tablespoons thyme leaves
- 120g (4¼oz) good-quality green olives, pitted
- 2 tablespoons unsalted butter, melted
- 80g (2¾oz) pickled caper shoots, or capers
- 6 tablespoons honey
- 50g (1¾oz) ricotta salata cheese (or use Parmesan), shaved, to garnish
- flaky sea salt and freshly ground black pepper

CHEESE SAUCE PIDE
WITH CHARRED LEEKS
& CRISPY POTATOES

MAKES 6

6 large leeks, dark green parts removed

3 large potatoes

sunflower oil, for frying

1 quantity Pide dough (see page 60)

2 tablespoons dried oregano

2 tablespoons sesame seeds, lightly toasted

2 tablespoons unsalted butter, melted

6 tablespoons tulum cheese (or use feta or a crumbly goats' cheese)

flaky sea salt

fine salt

FOR THE CHEESE SAUCE

65g (2½oz) unsalted butter

45g (1¾oz) plain flour

500ml (18fl oz) milk

50g (1¾oz) pecorino cheese (or any hard cheese), grated

85g (3oz) hellim cheese, grated

This *pide* is very subtle in its flavours. The cheese sauce is not too strong and provides a lovely creamy centre. You could also drizzle a little garlic oil over the leeks for an extra layer of flavour. Tulum is generally sold in jars and has a very strong, almost Parmesan-like flavour.

Preheat the oven to 240°C (475°F), Gas Mark 9. Put a pizza stone or a large flat baking tray in the oven.

———

First make the cheese sauce: melt the butter in a saucepan over a medium heat, then whisk in the flour. Add one-third of the milk and whisk until smooth. Add the remaining milk in 2 batches, whisking well each time. Turn the heat right down and cook gently for about 15 minutes, whisking occasionally. Finally, whisk in the cheese – the pecorino will melt, but the hellim won't. Transfer to a shallow tray and allow to cool completely.

———

Put the leeks on a baking tray and roast for about 20 minutes, turning halfway through, until the outside is charred. For a smoky flavour, the barbecue is the best place to cook them. Peel off the burnt outer layer of the leeks, leaving on a few of the charred bits, as they provide good flavour. Cut the leeks into 2cm (¾in) slices.

———

Slice the potatoes as finely as possible on a mandoline (watch your fingers!). Place in a bowl of warm water to remove excess starch, then lay them out to dry on a clean tea towel. Heat the oil in a deep-fat fryer to 160°C (325°F). Alternatively, heat a 2cm (¾in) depth of oil in a deep frying pan over a high heat. When hot enough, a small cube of bread added to the oil should sizzle immediately. Put a batch of potatoes in the fryer, one at a time to avoid them sticking together and fry until golden and crisp. Remove and drain on kitchen paper, then season with fine salt. Repeat with the remaining potatoes.

———

To make the pides (I suggest making them one at a time), roll out a ball of dough on a floured surface into a large oval shape about 40 x 15cm (16 x 6in). Spread one-sixth of the cheese sauce down the middle, leaving a 3cm (1¼in) border around the edge. Sprinkle over some dried oregano and sesame seeds and top with a layer of leeks, then season with flaky salt. Fold in the sides as shown on page 61, and pinch the ends together really well so that the pide doesn't unravel during baking.

———

Slide your pide onto a very flat baking sheet, then slide it onto the preheated baking tray or pizza stone. Bake for 10–12 minutes, or until golden brown and crisp on the outside. Remove and brush the sides with the melted butter. Add a line of crispy potatoes down the middle, then sprinkle over some tulum cheese. Make 5 more in the same way.

MEAT

BARBECUE CHICKEN WINGS WITH GARLIC & KAYSERI PASTIRMA DRESSING

150ml (5fl oz) extra-virgin olive oil, plus extra for the wings

8 slices Kayseri pastirma, sliced into 1cm (½in) strips

3 garlic cloves, thinly sliced

1 tablespoon thyme leaves

50ml (2fl oz) sherry vinegar

12 chicken wings, jointed into 2 pieces

small bunch of bunch flat leaf parsley, leaves shredded

flaky sea salt and freshly ground black pepper

Chicken wings are one of my absolute favourite foods. More and more restaurants are serving them in different guises, and this is my take on them. Kayseri pastirma is a type of really delicious air-dried beef coated in *çemen* (a Turkish spice paste, see page 199), and it's worth tracking down in your local Turkish supermarket. If you can't find it, Spanish *cecina* would be a good alternative, or you could use another cured meat, such as chorizo or salami, although the flavours wouldn't be quite the same. This dressing works very well with lots of things; in the restaurant we also use it with shellfish such as mussels and clams.

Heat a barbecue until the coals turn grey. Alternatively, heat the grill until medium-hot.

——

Pour the olive oil into a small pan, add the garlic and cook over a medium heat until it starts to turn golden brown. Add the pastirma and cook until it starts to turn crispy, then add the thyme and sherry vinegar. Remove from the heat, pour into a large bowl and leave to cool.

——

Coat the chicken wings in a little olive oil and season with salt and pepper. Cook on the barbecue or under the grill for about 15 minutes, turning them every 1–2 minutes to ensure even cooking. Once they are golden brown and cooked through, remove from the heat and immediately put them in the bowl with the dressing. Add the parsley, give it all a good toss and serve sprinkled with a little extra sea salt over the top.

CHICKEN LIVERS WITH GARLIC, ROSEMARY, CUMIN & DATE BUTTER ON TOAST

If you've already made the Medjool Date Butter (on page 186), this is a really quick and simple dish to throw together. The sweet, buttery sauce complements the iron-rich flavour of the chicken livers.

Toast the bread, either in a toaster or under a hot grill, then set aside.

───

Heat the olive oil in a large frying pan over a high heat and add the chicken livers. Sauté them for 1–2 minutes if you like them pink in the middle; if you prefer them cooked through, sauté for 4–5 minutes. Add the garlic, rosemary and cumin and cook for another minute or so, or until the garlic starts to brown.

───

Remove the pan from the heat and add the date butter, according to taste. Gently stir until melted, then season with salt. Add the parsley and divide the mixture between the slices of toast.

SERVES 4

4 slices white crusty bread

2 tablespoons olive oil

500g (1lb 2oz) chicken livers, trimmed and sinews removed

2 garlic cloves, thinly sliced

1 large sprig of rosemary, finely chopped

1 teaspoon ground cumin

2–3 heaped tablespoons Medjool Date Butter (see page 186)

small handful flat leaf parsley leaves, chopped

flaky sea salt

SALAD OF BAHARAT-ROAST DUCK WITH FETA, SUMAC ONIONS, POACHED FIGS & SALTED WALNUTS

I started out using *baharat* only in bread, but soon discovered how versatile this spice mixture is, and now use it in all sorts of dishes, including meat and fish recipes. If you don't have time to make your own using the recipe in this book, you can buy it from most Turkish supermarkets.

Preheat the oven to 200°C (400°F), Gas Mark 6. Alternatively, if you have a barbecue that can cook things slowly, cook it on that for extra flavour.

——

Rub the duck with a little olive oil, the baharat and salt. Place it upside down in a roasting tin and roast for 1 hour. Carefully drain off any excess oil from the tin and turn the duck over. Return to the oven for 1 more hour. Remove the duck and leave it to rest and cool a little. Reduce the oven temperature to 170°C (325°F), Gas Mark 3.

——

Meanwhile, put the water in a small pan, add the sugar, star anise and vinegar, and bring to the boil. Continue boiling to reduce the liquid by half. Add the figs, cut-side down, and cook gently for 4–5 minutes, or until they collapse just a little. Remove the figs and leave them to cool to room temperature.

To make the walnuts, whisk the egg white with the icing sugar, salt and some black pepper until a little frothy. Add the walnuts and coat well. Place on a baking tray lined with baking parchment and bake for 5–10 minutes, or until crisp and golden.

——

In a small bowl, mix together the onion and sumac with a pinch of salt. Massage them together a little and set aside. Tear the duck into pieces; it is up to you whether you would like it off the bone or not. Season the duck with salt.

——

Place the salad leaves in a serving bowl along with the figs, mint leaves, onions and feta, and mix gently. To serve, place a few pieces of duck on a plate, add some salad and scatter over some walnuts. Drizzle over some olive oil and a squeeze of lemon to finish.

SERVES 4–6

1 free-range duck, giblets removed

extra-virgin olive oil, for rubbing and drizzling

2 tablespoons baharat (see page 193; also available in Turkish supermarkets)

150ml (5fl oz) water

50g (1¾oz) caster sugar

1 star anise

1½ tablespoons sherry vinegar or red wine vinegar

4 figs, cut in half

1 red onion, thinly sliced

2 tablespoons sumac

150g (5½oz) mixed salad leaves

leaves from 4 sprigs of mint

120g (4¼oz) Turkish white cheese or feta

1 lemon

flaky sea salt and freshly ground black pepper

FOR THE WALNUTS

1 large egg white

20g (¾oz) icing sugar

1 teaspoon flaky sea salt

125g (4½oz) walnuts

GRILLED QUAILS WITH A PALM SUGAR, SUMAC & OREGANO GLAZE

This was one of the first recipes I created when working for Peter Gordon at The Providores. I'd never cooked with palm sugar before I worked there and it was really exciting to experiment with this new ingredient. The birds are definitely best cooked on the barbecue, but if the weather isn't on your side, you can also cook them under a grill or in the oven.

Heat a barbecue until the coals have turned grey, or preheat a grill.

———

Mix together the palm sugar, sumac, oregano and olive oil. Pour half the mixture over the quails and leave to marinate for at least 1 hour. Season the quails with salt and pepper and place them on the barbecue or under the grill skin-side down. Make sure the coals are not too hot, or you may burn the skin. After 1 minute, turn the quails over, then turn every minute or so until they are cooked to your liking. I like to keep mine a little pink, so I cook them for 6–8 minutes. Just before removing them, brush with the remaining marinade and cook for another minute.

———

Remove the quails from the barbecue and leave to rest for about 5 minutes. Serve with the caper dressing.

SERVES 4

2 tablespoons palm sugar, pounded finely using a pestle and mortar

2 tablespoons sumac

1 tablespoon dried oregano

6 tablespoons extra-virgin olive oil

4 quails, spatchcocked

flaky sea salt and freshly ground black pepper

Caper Dressing (see page 194), to serve

CHILLI-GARLIC GLAZED CHICKEN WITH ZA'ATAR CRUMBS

This recipe was designed for the press launch of Oklava, held on a rooftop in east London. Conscious of the press's power to make or break a new restaurant, I was keen to create the best chicken dish I could, something that would stick in the memory of the journalists and critics attending. Torn between developing a smoky barbecued chicken and a crispy fried chicken, I came up with this recipe, which combines the best of both. It's sticky, smoky, crispy and thoroughly messy to eat, especially if, as I do, you prefer to get stuck in with your hands. Although the recipe tells you how to make this in the oven, it's really best cooked over a barbecue for added smokiness, so if the sun is shining, get outside and cook al fresco. Serve with Lime Mayonnaise (see page 188).

SERVES 4–6

1 medium free-range chicken, cut into 10 pieces through the bone

olive oil, for drizzling

1 lime, cut into wedges

FOR THE BRINE

1 litre (1¾ pints) cold water

50g (1¾oz) fine salt

1 teaspoon sweet smoked paprika

FOR THE GLAZE

3 red chillies

15 garlic cloves

325g (11½oz) palm sugar

50g (1¾oz) Turkish hot pepper paste (açi biber salçasi)

165ml (5½fl oz) cider vinegar

FOR THE ZA'ATAR CRUMBS

80g (2¾oz) za'atar

30g (1oz) sesame seeds, lightly toasted

20g (¾oz) sumac

300g (10½oz) dried breadcrumbs

flaky sea salt

Preheat the oven to 160°C (325°F), Gas Mark 3. Remove the skin from all the chicken pieces except the wings. Put it on a baking tray and bake for about 30 minutes, or until golden and crisp, draining off the fat a few times during cooking. Once the skin has cooled, chop it finely. Turn the oven up to 240°C (475°F), Gas Mark 9.

To make the brine, bring 200ml (7fl oz) of the water to the boil with the salt and paprika. Tip it into a bowl and add the remaining cold water. Place the chicken pieces in a bowl, pour the brine over them and refrigerate for 3 hours. Rinse the chicken under cold water and pat dry.

To make the glaze, roughly chop the chillies and garlic. Put them in a food processor and blend to a coarse purée. Put the palm sugar in a saucepan over a medium heat and leave to caramelize. As soon as that happens, add the chilli and garlic purée and hot pepper paste. Cook over a medium heat for about 5 minutes. Finally, add the cider vinegar and continue to cook for 15–20 minutes, or until the glaze has a syrupy consistency.

To make the crumbs, combine the ingredients in a bowl and stir in the crispy chicken skin. Tip the mixture onto a large tray.

Put the chicken pieces on a large baking tray, well spaced, and drizzle with a little olive oil. Bake for about 15 minutes, or until two-thirds cooked. Remove from the oven and generously ladle the glaze over all the pieces. Return to the oven for 5 minutes, then remove and repeat the glazing process. Once the chicken is cooked through and well glazed, remove from the oven and put the pieces straight into the tray of za'atar crumbs. Coat them well and serve with the lime mayonnaise and wedges of lime on the side.

BEEF MEATBALLS IN SOUR CHERRY SAUCE WITH BULGUR WHEAT PILAV

SERVES 6

750g (1lb 10oz) minced beef

1 tablespoon baharat (see page 193; also available in Turkish supermarkets)

1 tablespoon Turkish chilli flakes (pul biber)

100ml (3½fl oz) extra-virgin olive oil

3 onions, chopped

2 tablespoons thyme, leaves removed

1 heaped teaspoon sweet pepper paste (tatli biber salçasi)

1kg (2lb 4oz) red cherries, pitted

freshly squeezed juice of 1 lemon

40g (1½oz) cold unsalted butter, diced

small bunch of flat leaf parsley, chopped

fine salt

flaky sea salt and freshly ground black pepper

FOR THE BULGUR PILAV

2 tablespoons extra-virgin olive oil

1 onion, chopped

1 tablespoon sweet pepper paste (tatli biber salçasi)

400g (14oz) tinned tomatoes or 2 ripe tomatoes, chopped

300ml (10fl oz) stock or water

200g (7oz) coarse bulgur wheat

fine salt

FOR THE FENNEL YOGURT

6 heaped tablespoons Turkish or Greek yogurt

1 tablespoon ground fennel

I first had this dish at Ciya Sofrasi in Istanbul, where the chef is known for recreating Ottoman dishes and incorporating wild ingredients into his food. This is my version of a classic. If you can't find fresh cherries, frozen will work well too. And if you can't find *tatli biber salçasi*, a type of Turkish sweet pepper paste, use tomato purée instead.

Start by mixing the minced beef with the baharat and chilli flakes and season with fine salt. Cook a little in a frying pan to check the seasoning, then adjust the mixture as necessary. Knead the mixture very well, then shape it into small meatballs about 2cm (¾in) in diameter. Chill until needed.

———

Heat the olive oil in a large shallow saucepan over a medium heat and add the onions. Gently cook until soft, about 15 minutes. Add the thyme leaves and sweet pepper paste and continue to cook for 2 minutes. Now add the meatballs, half the cherries and enough water to come halfway up the meatballs. Season with salt and pepper, give it a gentle stir, then cover and turn the heat right down. Cook for 30 minutes, stirring occasionally.

———

Meanwhile, make the bulgur pilav. Heat the olive oil in a small saucepan, add the onion and cook gently over a medium heat for about 10 minutes. Add the sweet pepper paste and cook for 1 more minute. Add the tomatoes, stock or water and bulgur wheat and a little fine salt. Stir well, increase the heat and bring to the boil. Turn the heat right down, then cover and cook for 8–10 minutes, or until the liquid is absorbed. Remove from the heat, place a piece of kitchen paper directly on the bulgur wheat, and put the lid on again. Set aside.

———

Mix together the yogurt and ground fennel. Season with flaky salt.

———

To finish the meatballs, add the remaining cherries, the lemon juice and butter. Cook for 5–10 minutes, or until you have a nice sauce consistency. Turn the heat off and add the parsley. Check the seasoning and serve with the pilav and fennel yogurt.

VEAL SHISH & ONION SALAD FLATBREAD WITH CHARRED SIVRI BIBER RELISH & YOGURT

For many people, veal remains a dirty word. British rose veal from dairy farm bull calves is, however, an ethically sourced, high-welfare product with a delicate flavour. It's perfect in this flatbread recipe. I like to cook everything on a barbecue, but you can use a hot griddle pan if you prefer. The breads could even be cooked in an oven preheated too 240°C (475°F), Gas Mark 9.

Heat a barbecue until the coals turn grey.

———

Put the veal in a bowl with the chilli flakes, cumin, oregano and half the olive oil. Leave it to marinate in the refrigerator for a minimum of 2 hours, preferably overnight.

———

If you are making your own flatbreads, punch down the dough and and divide it into 8–10 equal pieces, depending on how big you want to make them. Lightly flour a work surface and roll out one piece at a time into a long oval shape about 4mm (⅛in) thick. As you roll them, place directly on the hot barbecue rack, griddle pan or oven shelf (make sure the bars aren't too wide apart) and cook for about 1 minute on each side, or until a little puffed up and charred. Set aside and keep warm.

———

To make the relish, put the peppers on the barbecue (or in the griddle pan) and cook, turning them occasionally, until blackened all over. Remove and leave to cool. Once cool enough to handle, tear the tops off and strip away most of the skin, but don't remove all the charred bits. Chop the flesh into small pieces. Place in a bowl and mix with the spring onions, coriander, lemon juice and olive oil. Season with salt and pepper.

———

To make the onion salad, separate the onion layers, push them onto metal skewers and place on the barbecue. Cook for 2–3 minutes, turning now and then, until charred on both sides. Remove from the skewer and put them in a bowl with the pomegranate molasses, turnip juice, olive oil, parsley and sumac. Season with salt and pepper and give it a good mix.

———

Finally, thread the veal pieces onto metal skewers and grill for about 3 minutes on each side, or until golden brown. Season them with fine salt during cooking. Place the skewers straight on the flatbreads to rest and release their juices for 5 minutes. To serve, spread some yogurt on a flatbread and top with the veal, onion salad and pepper relish.

SERVES 6

750g (1lb 10oz) rose veal shoulder, leg or sirloin, cut into 3cm (1¼in) cubes

1 tablespoon urfa chilli flakes (isot biber)

1 tablespoon ground cumin

1 tablespoon dried oregano

100ml (3½fl oz) extra-virgin olive oil

1 quantity Pide dough (see page 60) or 4 good-quality flatbreads

flour, for dusting

4 tablespoons Turkish or Greek yogurt

FOR THE SIVRI BIBER RELISH

8 hot Turkish peppers (sivri biber; use green chillies if you can't find them)

4 spring onions, thinly sliced

small bunch of coriander, leaves and stalks, chopped

freshly squeezed juice of 1 lemon

50ml (2fl oz) extra-virgin olive oil

flaky sea salt and freshly ground pepper

FOR THE ONION SALAD

2 onions, quartered

2 tablespoons pomegranate molasses

4 teaspoons turnip juice (salgam)

50ml (2fl oz) extra-virgin olive oil

small bunch of flat leaf parsley, leaves only

1 tablespoon sumac

RUMP STEAK TANTUNI WITH RED ONION, PEPPER & PARSLEY SALAD

SERVES 2

2 tablespoons Turkish or Greek yogurt

1 tablespoon Turkish hot pepper paste (açi biber salçasi)

1 tablespoon extra-virgin olive oil

2 rump steaks, about 250g (9oz) each

2–3 tablespoons sunflower oil

1 Turkish loaf (somun) or a baguette

1–2 teaspoons urfa chilli flakes (isot biber)

1–2 teaspoons sweet smoked paprika

2 plum tomatoes, peeled and diced

2 long green Turkish peppers (Charleston peppers; use ordinary peppers if you can't find them), sliced

flaky sea salt

FOR THE SALAD

1 small red onion, thinly sliced

2 tablespoons sumac

small bunch of flat leaf parsley, leaves only, shredded

I came up with this recipe for Soho Food Feast, a fundraising fête held every year at Soho Parish Primary School in central London. A number of London restaurants set up food stalls at this amazing event, which also features live music, a raffle and the always-hilarious children's vegetable sculpture competition. *Tantuni,* **from the port city of Mersin in southeast Turkey, is traditionally made with boiled beef or chicken but I prefer to use fried steak as a Turkish take on the classic British steak sandwich.**

Mix the yogurt with the hot pepper paste and olive oil. Smear this all over the steaks and leave to marinate in the refrigerator for 2 hours (remove them 30 minutes before cooking).

———

Heat 1½ tablespoons of the sunflower oil in a large frying pan. Season the steaks with salt and fry for 2–3 minutes on each side, until a caramelized crust forms. Remove from the pan and leave to rest for 10 minutes. Clean the pan with kitchen paper and set aside.

———

Meanwhile, make the salad. Mix the onion with the sumac and parsley. Season with flaky sea salt and set aside until needed.

———

Dice the steaks into roughly 1cm (½in) pieces. Split the bread lengthways, not quite cutting all the way through, and trim it so that it will eventually fit into the frying pan. Heat the remaining oil in the empty pan until it is very hot. Add the diced meat, chilli flakes and paprika, and fry for 2 minutes, then add about 3 tablespoons water and a little more salt. Scrape any sticky bits off the bottom of the pan, then put the bread cut-side down on top of the meat and push it right down so it soaks up all the juices from the pan.

———

To serve, put the bread on a chopping board and scoop all the meat onto it. Top with the onion salad, tomatoes and peppers. Season with a little extra salt, then cut in half and serve.

ARTICHOKE & BEEF DOLMA

This is another of my mum's recipes, and a regular feature on our Sunday dinner table. While writing this book, I've often called my mum to check the ingredients and techniques of some of her favourite dishes. At times this has been difficult – the recipes are second nature to her, so she'd tell me to put 'some' of this, 'a bit' of that and 'not too much' of the other. Mum doesn't use measurements, so getting to the end result you see in this book hasn't always been straightforward. With this dish, though, it can be particularly difficult to get the quantities right, as each artichoke will be a different size, making it tricky to know exactly how much filling you'll need. I always make extra, as this mixture also works well stuffed into potatoes, peppers, courgettes or just about any vegetable you fancy.

SERVES 8

8 globe artichokes

freshly squeezed juice of
  2–3 lemons

50ml (2fl oz) extra-virgin
  olive oil

2 onions, diced

1kg (2lb 4oz) minced beef

1 tablespoon tomato purée

400g (14oz) tinned tomatoes,
  or 4 fresh tomatoes,
  chopped

250g (9oz) long-grain rice,
  rinsed

large bunch of flat leaf
  parsley, chopped (a little
  stalk is good)

8 large slices tomato

flaky sea salt and freshly
  ground black pepper

Cut the stalks off the artichokes and remove the chokes, using a small knife and a spoon as shown in the photographs. Put in a bowl of water with the juice of 1 lemon.

—

Heat the oil in a large pan, add the onions and cook gently for about 15 minutes, or until translucent. Add the minced beef and cook until it takes on a little colour, about 15 minutes. Break up the mince thoroughly as it cooks. Add the tomato purée and tomatoes and cook the mixture over a medium heat for a further 20 minutes. Season with salt and pepper. Add the rice and cook for another 5 minutes. Turn the heat off, add the parsley and the juice of 1 lemon (or more if you like it very lemony) and leave to cool. Meanwhile. preheat the oven to 190°C (375°F), Gas Mark 5.

—

Once the filling has cooled, drain the artichokes and pat dry with kitchen paper. Spoon the filling into the hollows, then place the artichokes on a baking tray that holds them snugly. Top each one with a slice of tomato. Fill the tray halfway up with water, cover tightly with kitchen foil and bake for about 1 hour, or until the rice is cooked through. Remove the foil and bake for a further 10 minutes. Set aside and allow to cool a little before serving.

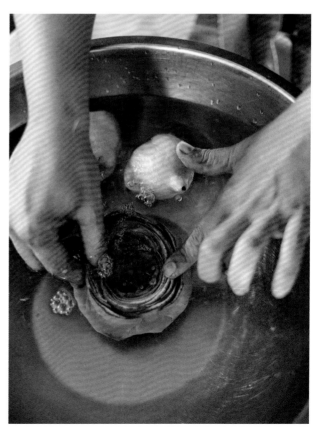

ÇEMEN-BRAISED SHORT RIBS
WITH BROWN BUTTER BREAD SAUCE

Çemen is a Turkish spice paste used to make Kayseri pastirma, but it is also served as a meze to be spread onto bread. If you don't want to make your own (see page 199), you can buy it from a Turkish supermarket. This dish is delicious served with Tomato-Pomegranate Salad (see page 16) to cut through the richness of the sauce. I also recommend serving it with melted Chilli Butter (see page 186), as shown here.

Preheat the oven to 180°C (350°F), Gas Mark 4. Put the short ribs in a roasting tin that fits them snugly and tuck the onion around them. Whisk the çemen with a little water to form a loose paste. Pour it into the tin and top up with just enough water to submerge the ribs. Cover with foil and bake for 3–4 hours, or until the meat is just coming away from the bone.

———

Meanwhile, make the bread sauce. Heat half the oil in a pan over a low heat, add the shallot and garlic and cook for about 5 minutes, or until softened. In a separate pan, melt the butter over a medium heat and keep cooking until it turns a nut-brown colour. Strain it through a fine sieve lined with kitchen paper. Add the breadcrumbs to the shallots, followed by the milk. Gently cook over a low heat, stirring until thickened. Add the double cream and season with salt. Finally, whisk in the browned butter. If you prefer, you could blend the sauce until completely smooth.

———

Once the ribs are cooked, pour the cooking liquid into a pan and reduce over a high heat until it reaches a gravy-like consistency. This might take a while, depending how much liquid you have. Remove and discard any bones or gristle from the meat. Wrap each rib tightly in clingfilm and leave to cool in the refrigerator. Meanwhile, melt the chilli butter, if using, and keep warm.

———

Once cool, cut each rib into 5 slices. Heat the remaining sunflower oil in a large frying pan. Add the rib slices and fry on each side until browned. Add some of the reduced meat sauce and turn the heat down. Cook the slices in the sauce until glazed (you might need to do this in a few batches).

———

To serve, reheat the bread sauce if necessary. Spoon it onto plates, place the beef on the sauce and add a little drizzle of extra sauce over the top. Pour over some warm chilli butter, if using.

SERVES 4

4 beef short ribs on the bone, about 12cm (4½in) long

1 onion, sliced

2 tablespoons çemen

½ quantity Chilli Butter (see page 186), to serve (optional)

FOR THE BREAD SAUCE

2 tablespoons sunflower oil

1 shallot, diced

2 garlic cloves, grated

100g (3½oz) unsalted butter

100g (3½oz) fresh white breadcrumbs

500ml (18 fl oz) milk

80ml (2¾oz) double cream

flaky sea salt

FRIED BEEF KÖFTE

4 potatoes, finely grated
    (any white potato is fine, but
    I like Cyprus potatoes)

600g (1lb 5oz) minced beef

2 small or 1 large onion, finely
    chopped

small bunch of flat leaf
    parsley, finely chopped

1 large egg

150–200g (5½–7oz) fresh
    white breadcrumbs (from
    a white crusty loaf, crusts
    removed)

vegetable oil, for frying

fine salt and freshly ground
    black pepper

This is a classic Cypriot *köfte*, just like my mum makes them. The addition of potato keeps them really moist in the middle and crispy on the outside. At home we would always have them with Turkish-style rice or Cyprus potato chips and a big bowl of chopped salad. When we have these on the menu in the restaurant I always serve them with Tomato Relish (see page 189) as a dip on the side. For best results, cook one *köfte* to check the seasoning before shaping and frying the rest.

Put the grated potatoes in a clean tea towel and squeeze with your hands to get rid of any excess liquid. Transfer to a large bowl and add all the remaining ingredients, except the oil, and season with salt and pepper. Knead the mixture for about 1 minute.

———

Pour enough oil into a frying pan to fill it no more than one-third full and place over a medium heat. When hot enough, a small cube of bread added to the oil should sizzle immediately. Alternatively, heat the oil in a deep-fat fryer.

———

Shape the beef mixture into köftes – either short, stumpy oval sausages (as is traditional) or small balls. It's easier to do this with damp hands. When the oil reaches 180°C (350°F), you can start frying.

———

Add as many köftes as your pan can hold, leaving a 2cm (¾in) gap between them. Cook until they have taken on a nice dark brown colour, then flip them over and cook the other side. Remove and drain on kitchen paper.

———

Continue to cook in batches until the mixture is used up. If you want to eat the köftes all at the same time, earlier batches can be reheated in a low oven. They can also be eaten warm or even cold.

SPICED BEEF & BULGUR WHEAT KÖFTES

This is my take on a traditional Cypriot dish that I learnt from one of my mum's friends. Traditionally, the dough is made with only bulgur wheat and water, but getting the consistency right can be challenging, which is why I've added eggs, flour and olive oil. You can add different spices and herbs to the meat to your liking, but it's important not to add more wet ingredients, or you are likely to end up with a cracked casing where the juices have run into the dough.

Start by making the dough. In a large, deep tray, combine the bulgur wheat and fine salt and add enough water to cover the bulgur wheat by about 1cm (½in); the wheat will start absorbing it immediately but you don't need to add more. Mix thoroughly, then cover with a clean cloth and leave to absorb all the liquid; this will take about 30 minutes.

—

Meanwhile, to make the filling, heat 2 tablespoons of the oil in a frying pan over a medium heat, add the onions and cook until lightly browned. Remove from the pan. Carefully wipe the pan out with kitchen paper and return it to a high heat.

—

Add the remaining olive oil and the mince, breaking it up in the pan. Fry until it has browned all over and any excess moisture has evaporated. This will take about 15 minutes. Return the onion to the pan and season with salt and pepper.

—

Now add the spices and cook for a few more minutes. Add the vinegar and sugar and cook for another minute. Remove from the heat and stir in the parsley. Check the seasoning and leave the mince to cool.

—

To finish the dough, add the egg, olive oil and 4 tablespoons flour to the soaked bulgur and knead by hand or using a stand mixer with the paddle attachment for at least 5–10 minutes, or until you can form it into a ball without it sticking to your hands. If you feel the mixture is too wet, add a little more flour.

—

Heat the oil in a deep-fat fryer to 180°C (350°F). Alternatively, place a deep frying pan over a high heat and add enough sunflower oil to cover the köftes. When hot enough, a small cube of bread added to the oil should sizzle immediately.

—

To shape the köftes, break off a piece of dough a bit bigger than a golf ball and roll into a ball. Using slightly wet hands, poke your finger in and start turning the dough, shaping it into a long pocket with 8mm (³/₈in) thick walls. Keep the top end a bit wider so that it is easier to stuff. Spoon in some of the beef filling, leaving about 1..5cm (⁵/₈in) empty at the top. Now close off the end and ensure there are no gaps in your dough. If there are any cracks, remould, adding extra dough if needed, and smooth it over with damp hands.

—

Carefully place a few köftes at a time in the hot oil and fry for about 5 minutes, or until dark golden brown. Repeat the process until all the mixture is used up. Serve with lemon wedges to squeeze into the filling.

MAKES 16–20

sunflower oil, for frying

1 lemon, cut into wedges

FOR THE DOUGH

250g (9oz) fine bulgur wheat

1 teaspoon fine salt

about 800ml (1½ pints) boiling water

1 medium egg

1 tablespoon extra-virgin olive oil

4–8 heaped tablespoons plain flour

yogurt with a drizzle of pomegranate molasses, to serve (optional)

FOR THE FILLING

4 tablespoons olive oil

2 onions, chopped

500g (1lb 2oz) minced beef

1 teaspoon ground cumin

1 teaspoon ground coriander

1 teaspoon sweet smoked paprika

1 tablespoon sherry vinegar

1 teaspoon caster sugar

small bunch of flat leaf parsley, finely shredded (a little stalk is good)

flaky sea salt and freshly ground black pepper

SPICED BRAISED OXTAIL WITH SHALLOTS

Oxtail is a delicious but under-used cut: when cooked slowly, it produces soft, melting meat that is perfect for this hearty dish. A tablespoon of *açi biber salçasi* (hot pepper paste) adds warmth, but if you're not a fan, replace it with more tomato purée. I like to serve this stew with mashed potatoes or a good loaf of crusty white bread to mop up the juices.

———

Preheat the oven to 180°C (350°F), Gas Mark 4. Place the oil in a flameproof casserole dish over a high heat. Season the oxtail and dust it in the flour. Add it to the dish and cook until dark brown on both sides. Remove and set aside. If the meat has released a lot of oil, remove some of it from the pan.

———

Add the whole shallots to the dish and turn the heat down to medium. Gently cook until golden brown; about 10 minutes. Add the bay leaf, spices, tomato purée and pepper paste and cook for another 5 minutes. Add the red wine and cook to reduce by half. Return the oxtail to the dish and add just enough water to cover it. Put the lid on and place in the oven for 2–3 hours, or until the meat is falling off the bone.

———

Remove the oxtail and place the dish over a high heat to reduce the cooking liquid to a thick sauce. Return the oxtail to the dish, check the seasoning and serve.

SERVES 2–4

2 tablespoons sunflower oil

4 slices oxtail, about 5cm (2in) thick

1 tablespoon plain flour

12 round shallots

1 bay leaf

1 teaspoon ground cumin

1 teaspoon ground cinnamon

1 star anise

1 tablespoon tomato purée

1 tablespoon Turkish hot pepper paste (açi biber salçasi)

125ml (4fl oz) red wine

flaky sea salt and freshly ground black pepper

FRIED BEEF & ALLSPICE KÖFTES

SERVES 4-6

60g (2¼oz) long-grain rice,
  rinsed in warm water

sunflower oil, for frying

2 onions, chopped

500g (1lb 2oz) minced beef

1 teaspoon ground allspice

1 teaspoon freshly ground
  black pepper

3 large eggs

plain flour, for dusting

fine salt

This dish is called *kadin budu koftesi* in Turkish, which means 'ladies' thighs meatballs'. I've heard that this is because the shape of these *köftes* resemble female legs, although whether this is truth or folktale, I really couldn't say. But I can tell you that they work well as a part of a meze spread, or served alongside a nice mixed salad.

Put the rice and water in a small saucepan. Season with a little salt and boil for 10-15 minutes, or until just cooked. Drain and set aside to cool.

———

Heat a little oil in a frying pan, add the onions and cook gently over a medium heat for about 10 minutes, or until soft. Add half the minced beef and continue to cook for 10-15 minutes, or until lightly browned. Set aside to cool.

———

In a large bowl, combine the remaining minced beef with the rice, allspice, black pepper, 1 egg and the cooked mince. Season with salt and knead for about 5-10 minutes, or until the ingredients are well incorporated and form a ball. Fry a little piece to check the seasoning, then adjust the remaining raw mixture as necessary. Divide it into 14 equal pieces, and shape each into an oval patty.

———

Heat a shallow depth of oil in a large frying pan. Beat the remaining eggs in a bowl. Dust each patty in flour, coat in the egg and place in the hot oil. Fry for 1½ minutes, or until golden on each side. Drain on kitchen paper and season with a little fine salt.

RABBIT FRITTERS

SERVES 6–8

1 rabbit, farmed or wild, jointed into 8 pieces

4 onions, chopped

200ml (7fl oz) red wine vinegar

200ml (7fl oz) extra-virgin olive oil

4 sprigs of thyme

1 sprig of rosemary

4 sprigs of flat leaf parsley, chopped

4 sprigs of tarragon, chopped

flaky sea salt and freshly ground black pepper

FOR THE BATTER

250g (9oz) plain flour, plus extra for rolling

1 tablespoon fast-action dried yeast

1 teaspoon caster sugar

2 tablespoons nigella seeds

about 400ml (14fl oz) sparkling water

fine salt

I discovered *lalangi* (rabbit fritters) while chatting to one of my mum's friends about Cypriot food. Traditionally, this is a very simple dish in which you boil a whole rabbit in water and coat the picked meat in batter. The cooking method I use comes from my mum. Back in Cyprus, my dad used to go out hunting and bring back wild hares and rabbits. Mum would use vinegar and herbs to tame the strong flavour of the wild meat, a technique that I've adopted for many of my gamey dishes. Serve with Black Olive & Pepper Tapenade (see page 189).

Preheat the oven to 180°C (350°F), Gas Mark 4. Put the rabbit in a roasting tray with 2 chopped onions, half the vinegar, half the olive oil, the thyme and rosemary. Season with salt and pepper. Cover the tray with foil and roast for 90 minutes, or until the rabbit is falling off the bone. Remove and set aside to cool.

———

Meanwhile, put the remaining onions with the remaning olive oil in a small saucepan over a medium heat and cook gently until caramelized; this will take 10–15 minutes. Add the remaining vinegar and allow it to bubble until there is almost no liquid left. Leave the onions to cool.

———

Once the rabbit is cool enough to handle, pick all the meat off the bones and shred it up a little. Drain off any liquor and onions from the rabbit and cook gently in a small pan until there is almost no liquid left. Add it to the caramelized onions.

———

Season the rabbit meat and add the parsley, tarragon and onions. Mix it well, then shape the rabbit mixture into small balls about 3cm (1¼in) in diameter.

———

To make the batter, put the flour in a bowl along with the yeast, sugar and nigella seeds. Gradually add the sparkling water, whisking continously. You are aiming for quite a thick batter, like one you would make for fish, so you might not need all the water. Finish by adding the salt and leave it to rest for 30 minutes.

———

Heat the oil in a deep-fat fryer to 180°C (350°F). Alternatively, heat a 4cm (1½in) depth of oil in a frying pan over a high heat. When hot enough, a small cube of bread added to the oil should sizzle immediately.

———

In batches of however many will comfortably fit in your fryer or pan, roll the balls of rabbit in flour, dip them in the batter, then carefully add to the hot oil. Fry until golden and crispy. Remove and drain on kitchen paper and season with fine salt. Repeat with the rest of the mixture.

CRISPY POMEGRANATE-GLAZED LAMB BREAST WITH YOGURT

Having initially created this dish in my days as head chef at Kopapa, I have since developed it as presented here. It was born out of my love for lamb, pomegranate molasses and yogurt, and started out as lamb ribs. However, after a chef overcooked them and they all fell off the bone, I decided it was even better as lots of bits of crispy lamb. At the restaurant we press the lamb under a weight overnight to help with portioning, but you don't have to do that if you don't want to; it is just as delicious as randomly shaped crispy chunks. The lamb is best prepared a day in advance.

Preheat the oven to 180°C (350°F), Gas Mark 4. Place the lamb breast, onion and bay leaf in a large roasting tray or ovenproof casserole dish. Add enough water to cover the lamb by about 2cm (¾in). Cover with foil or a lid and roast for about 3 hours. The lamb is ready when you can pull the bones away without any resistance. Set the lamb aside to cool, reserving the cooking liquid.

———

When the lamb is cool enough to handle, but not completely cold, remove as much meat as possible, discarding the bones and any cartilage. Place the meat in the fridge until the fat has set – preferably overnight. To achieve the neat cubes shown here, layer the lamb in a shallow rectangular tray – it should be tightly packed. Put another tray on top and weigh it down to press the lamb into shape. The next day, cut the meat into 2cm (¾in) cubes.

———

To make the sauce, preheat the oven to 190°C (375°F), Gas Mark 5. Put all the spices in a small roasting tray and toast them on the middle shelf for about 6 minutes. Discard any fat on the surface

of the reserved cooking liquid, then place in a small pan with the toasted spices, pomegranate molasses, cider vinegar and sugar. Allow this to simmer, stirring occasionally, until it has a consistency like single cream, then strain off and discard the spices.

———

Put the diced lamb in a dry frying pan over a medium-high heat and fry until crispy all over, turning occasionally and seasoning with sea salt as you go. Be aware that a lot of fat will come out and the pan may spit at you, so take care. The pieces of lamb will break up a little in the pan, but that's fine. You want some bits that are super crispy and some bits that are soft in the middle; this can take anything from 8–12 minutes. Transfer the lamb to a colander to drain, discarding the excess fat. Season with flaky sea salt.

———

To serve, place the yogurt in individual bowls or one big bowl. Place the lamb on top, pour over as much sauce as you like and sprinkle over the herbs.

SERVES 4

1 bone-in lamb breast, about 2 kg (4lb 8oz) – ask your butcher to cut it into 4 or 5 pieces to make it more manageable

1 large onion, thickly sliced

1 bay leaf

flaky sea salt

FOR THE SAUCE

¼ teaspoon black peppercorns

¼ teaspoon fennel seeds

¼ teaspoon coriander seeds

1 cinnamon stick

4 cloves

100ml (3½fl oz) pomegranate molasses

50ml (2fl oz) cider vinegar

25g (1fl oz) dark brown sugar

TO SERVE

4 heaped tablespoons Turkish or Greek yogurt

4 sprigs of mint, finely shredded

4 sprigs of flat leaf parsley, finely shredded

QUINCE & ROSEMARY-GLAZED LAMB RUMP

SERVES 4

100g (3½oz) quince paste (membrillo)

1 sprig of rosemary, stalks removed

1 tablespoon sherry vinegar

2 tablespoons sunflower oil

4 lamb rumps, 200g (7oz) each, fat cap lightly scored

1 heaped tablespoon unsalted butter

flaky sea salt and freshly ground black pepper

I have to restrain myself from putting too many lamb dishes on the menu. As a Turk, I guess this love affair with lamb is quite natural. Lamb rump, sometimes also known as chump, is an underused cut, which is a great shame as it is full of flavour. Try to buy your rumps of lamb from a butcher, if you can, as supermarkets tend to sell them in slices rather than lovely hunks of meat. This recipe would work really well served with roast potatoes and vegetables, but it can also be served alongside other dishes for sharing. You could try the glaze with a leg of lamb instead of rumps – in which case preheat the oven to 200°C (400°F), Gas Mark 6 and roast for 25 minutes for every 450g (1lb) of lamb. Increase the temperature to 220°C (425°F), Gas Mark 7, and pour on the glaze. Return to the oven for 10 minutes, or until caramelized, basting halfway through the cooking time.

Preheat the oven to 220°C (425°F), Gas Mark 7. In a small blender, process the quince paste, rosemary, sherry vinegar and 3 tablespoons water until smooth.

———

Heat the oil into a large ovenproof frying pan over a medium heat. Season the lamb rumps with salt and pepper and put them in the pan, fat-side down. Cook for about 5 minutes, or until golden. Increase the heat and turn them over. Brown them on all sides, then turn them fat-side down again. Transfer the pan to the oven and roast for 5 minutes. Turn the lamb rumps over and return to the oven for 3 minutes. Remove and allow to rest for at least 10 minutes. The meat will be pink in the middle; if you prefer it well cooked, just leave it in the oven for a bit longer.

———

Once the lamb has rested, put the pan over a high heat. Add the lamb rumps, about 50ml (2fl oz) of the glaze and add the butter. You can add all the glaze if you like this dish extra sticky, or save the rest to use another time, as it keeps well in the fridge. Let the glaze bubble up, turning until it is well coated. Remove the lamb and leave to cool slightly. Once cool enough to handle, slice each rump into 4 or 5 slices. Pour over any pan juices and sprinkle over some flaky sea salt to serve.

SPICED FRIED CRISPY LAMB'S LIVER

SERVES 4

250g (9oz) lamb's liver, membranes removed

250ml (9oz) milk

1 tablespoon ground fennel

1 tablespoon ground cumin

1 tablespoon sweet smoked paprika

1 tablespoon urfa chilli flakes (isot biber)

120g (4¼oz) plain flour

1 tablespoon fine salt, plus extra for seasoning

sunflower oil, for frying

Laura and I first tried this dish while in Turkey before the opening of Oklava. We had spent a lovely night at Arcadia vineyard, and on the way back to Istanbul our hosts took us to a restaurant in Edirne, close to the borders with Greece and Bulgaria. Edirne is famous for its thinly sliced fried lamb's liver and we were keen to try it out. Our hosts ordered what turned out to be huge plates of the dish, which I excitedly tucked into, relishing the rich flavour. If you're an offal fan like me, you'll love this simple dish, which I've adapted with the addition of a few spices. If you can't find urfa chilli flakes, use normal chilli flakes instead. Serve with tomatoes, raw onions, lettuce and bread and Fried Dried Chilli Yogurt (see page 199).

Slice the liver into very thin strips about 3mm (¹/₈in) thick. Soak it in the milk for about 1 hour. Mix all the spices together in a small bowl. Mix the flour with the measured salt.

———

Heat a 1cm (½in) depth of oil in a shallow frying pan over a medium heat. Take the liver slices out of the milk in small batches and coat them thoroughly in the seasoned flour. You can place the liver slices in a sieve to shake off any excess flour.

———

Lower the slices into the hot oil, ensuring they are well separated, and fry for 1–2 minutes, or until crisp and golden. Drain on kitchen paper and season with salt and the spice mixture.

FAMILY KEBABS

Even if I've just eaten dinner, the smell of kebabs makes me hungry again – it is probably my favourite meal. I'm not talking kebabs from your local takeaway, I'm talking about ones you will find, mostly on a Sunday, in pretty much every Turkish household.

Eating kebabs is a big social occasion. When I was growing up, I remember being excited when I knew we were having kebabs, not only because I loved them but also because it meant that all my cousins would be coming round to play. Kebabs are cooked on a barbecue, and the ultimate barbecues are held on the beach. The beach is a 5-minute drive from where my grandparents live in Cyprus, and families gather there every weekend to have their own barbecue or order kebabs from one of the beach shacks. It's a day of pure indulgence for me, consisting of sea, sunshine, sand and the smell of kebabs wafting from every direction. Here is what a typical barbecue at the Kiazim household consists of: Şeftali, Adana Köfte with Pitta Bread, Spicy Tomato Sauce and Yogurt, Lamb Shish, Lamb Chops, Chicken Pieces, my Mum's Hummus and Pilav, Cyprus Potato Salad and Shepherd's Salad.

LAMB SHISH

In our household we often use lamb leg meat for shish, but you could also use shoulder, depending on how much the fat content worries you. Dice the lamb into about 2cm (¾in) cubes, trimming it of any sinew and excessive fat (although a few cubes of fat skewered along with the meat is a good thing). Marinate the lamb for at least 2 hours, preferably overnight, in good olive oil and dried oregano (preferably wild oregano, known as kekik in Turkish, which has a more perfumed flavour). Place the meat on skewers and cook over very hot charcoals, seasoning with fine salt as you go.

LAMB CHOPS

You can grill lamb cutlets, which are delicious, but I prefer to use middle-neck lamb chops, mainly because I like getting stuck in and trying to get all the bits of meat off the bone. You will need to ask your butcher to cut these for you. Grill the chops over hot coals, seasoning with fine salt as you go, and turning them regularly to ensure they cook evenly.

CHICKEN PIECES

Joint a chicken into 8–10 pieces through the bone (your butcher can do this for you). I prefer to leave the skin on. Marinate it in good olive oil, lemon and dried oregano for at least 4 hours. Cook over medium-hot coals, seasoning with fine salt as you go, and turning it regularly to make sure the chicken cooks evenly and doesn't burn.

ADANA KÖFTE WITH PITTA BREAD, SPICY TOMATO SAUCE & YOGURT

SERVES 6

900g (2lb) minced lamb or beef

100g (3½oz) lamb suet (optional), frozen and finely grated

1 onion, finely chopped

large bunch of flat leaf parsley, finely chopped (a little stalk is good)

15g (½oz) fine salt

1 quantity Spicy Tomato Sauce (page 34), made without the bread

6 heaped tablespoons Turkish or Greek yogurt

6 pitta breads

freshly ground black pepper

This simple, classic kebab is named after the fifth largest city in Turkey. It works well as a meal in itself and is a favourite of my sister Sinem, who will sometimes light the barbecue mid-week just to make it. For an added bit of luxury, serve with Chilli Butter (see page 186) drizzled over the top.

Start by making the köfte. Combine the mince, suet, onion, parsley and salt. Add pepper to taste and knead well for 5–10 minutes. Divide into 85g (3oz) pieces and shape into small oval patties. Chill the köftes until needed.

Heat a barbecue until the coals turn grey, then grill the köftes over medium-hot coals, seasoning with a little fine salt and turning them regularly. If you have a metal grill for sandwiching fish on the barbecue, I would recommend using that. If not, just be careful when turning them over.

Grill the pitta breads on the barbecue and cut them into strips, then add some tomato sauce, pile on the köftes and top with yogurt.

ŞEFTALI

Şeftali was probably one of the first things I planned to put on the menu at Oklava, first because it's a Cypriot kebab, and second because it's my favourite! You must eat it with an onion salad, lavash or Turkish bread to absorb the juices, and lots of lemon. I have given specific measurements for the onion and parsley because for me it is very important to have the correct quantities, and every bunch of parsley or onion weighs a different amount.

Mix together the beef, onion, parsley, salt, chilli flakes and lamb suet. Knead for 5–10 minutes, or until well combined. Divide the mixture into 85g (3oz) pieces and shape each one into a sausage about 7cm (2¾in) long.

———

To wrap the şeftali, stretch a large piece of caul fat over a chopping board. Place a sausage on one corner of the board and cut the caul fat around it, leaving a 1.5cm (¾in) margin on 3 sides and leaving it at least 10cm (4in) long on the fourth side, Roll the caul fat around the sausage 1.5 times, tucking in the margins as you go. Repeat with the rest of the sausages.

———

Thread the sausages onto 2 large skewers, weaving them in and out to prevent them unravelling. Alternatively, if you have metal grill for sandwiching fish on the barbecue, you can line them up in that. Cook over medium-hot coals, seasoning with a little fine salt during cooking, and turning them regularly.

MAKES 18

900g (2lb) minced beef

450g (1lb) onion, finely chopped

300g (10½oz) flat leaf parsley, finely chopped (a little stalk is good)

15g (½oz) fine salt

40g (1½oz) Turkish chilli flakes (pul biber)

200g (7oz) lamb suet, frozen and finely grated

2–3kg (4lb 8oz–6lb 8oz) lamb caul fat, soaked in cold water with the juice of 1 lemon for 1 hour

MUM'S HUMMUS

Every Middle Eastern cook has their own recipe for making hummus and thinks theirs is the best. My mum's isn't fancy, but it's what I grew up with, so to me it is the best. She would always get me to taste it while she was making it and ask me, 'More garlic? More lemon?' Feel free to be flexible with the recipe, adding more or less tahini, garlic, lemon, pul biber or olive oil as you wish. I like it pretty lemony and garlicky.

Put the chickpeas, tahini, garlic, olive oil, chilli flakes and 2 tablespoons of water in a food processor and blend to a coarse purée. Add the lemon juice and check the seasoning.

———

Place in your serving bowl and garnish with olive oil, sumac and parsley.

SERVES 6–8

800g (1lb 12oz) tinned chickpeas, drained and rinsed

75g (2¾oz) tahini

1–2 garlic cloves

2 tablespoons extra-virgin olive oil, plus extra for drizzling

½–1 teaspoon Turkish chilli flakes (pul biber)

freshly squeezed juice of 1–2 lemons

sumac, to garnish

flat leaf parsley, chopped, to garnish

fine salt, to taste

MUM'S PILAV

Many people find cooking rice tricky, but the two top tips I learnt from my mum work a treat every time: always rinse the rice really well, then follow the rule of two parts water to one part rice. Rice cooked like this was a staple in our household as it goes really well with stew-style dishes (known as *yahni* in Turkish).

Heat the oil in a medium saucepan, add the onion and cook for a few minutes, until softened. If the vermicelli pasta is in nests, break them into small pieces and add to the pan. Cook until slightly golden. Add the rice and stir to coat in the oil for 1 minute.

———

Add the stock, season with salt, bring to the boil and give it one last stir. Turn the heat down to a low simmer, then cover and cook for about 15 minutes, or just until the water has evaporated. Remove from the heat and uncover, place a few sheets of kitchen paper over the top and put the lid back on. Leave to stand for 10 minutes before serving.

SERVES 6–8

1 tablespoon extra-virgin olive oil

1 small white onion, chopped

125g (4½oz) vermicelli pasta

500g (1lb 2oz) long-grain rice, rinsed thoroughly in warm water

1 litre (1¾ pints) boiling chicken or vegetable stock (I always follow the rule of 1 part rice to 2 parts liquid)

fine salt

SHEPHERD'S SALAD

SERVES 6–8

4 plum tomatoes, cut into 1cm (½in) dice

1 large onion, finely diced

1 cucumber, cut into 1cm (½in) dice

small bunch of flat leaf parsley, finely chopped

freshly squeezed juice of 1 lemon

fine salt

Known as *çoban salata* in Turkish, this salad goes well with every type of kebab as it is so refreshing and zingy. Sometimes when we're short of time we will just make some lamb shish and stuff them into pitta bread with this salad – a perfect mid-week meal.

Put all the ingredients in a bowl, mix well and season with salt.

CYPRUS POTATO SALAD WITH ROMAINE LETTUCE, HERBS, SPRING ONIONS, LEMON & OLIVE OIL

SERVES 6–8

8 Cyprus potatoes, scrubbed but not peeled

4 leaves Romaine lettuce, shredded

5 spring onions, thinly sliced

small bunch of flat leaf parsley, chopped (a little stalk is good)

small bunch of coriander, chopped, with stalks

small bunch of mint, leaves only, shredded

freshly squeezed juice of 2 lemons

100ml (3½fl oz) extra-virgin olive oil

flaky sea salt and freshly ground black pepper

Cyprus potatoes are some of the best in the world due to the incredible red soil they are grown in. They have a great flavour and a waxy consistency that works especially well for potato salads, so I would recommend trying to hunt them down for this recipe. If you can't find them, use another variety of waxy potato.

Put the whole potatoes into a large pan of cold salted water. Bring to a gentle simmer over a medium heat. Cook until just tender – about 30 minutes, depending on size. Once cooked, drain and leave to cool. Peel the potatoes and cut them into 2cm (¾in) dice. Mix all the ingredients together and season with salt and pepper.

SEAFOOD

TARAMA WITH FRIED MUSSELS & MINT OIL

In Istanbul there are lots of street vendors selling little skewers of battered fried mussels served with *tarator*, a sauce made with walnuts. Proper *tarama*, as opposed to the neon pink stuff sold in supermarkets, is a thing of real beauty. I would recommend making it even if you don't have time to make the whole dish. It's wonderful served with warm flatbread, or even chargrilled toast.

First make the tarama: start by peeling off and discarding the skin from the cod's roe. Put the roe in a small blender with the garlic, half the lemon juice, the soaked bread and the water. Blend until smooth. With the machine running, gradually add both the oils. (This process can also be done with hand-held electric beaters.) If the mixture gets too stiff, add a little warm water to bring it to the right consistency, then continue to add the oils. Taste to check the seasoning; add a little flaky salt if needed and more lemon juice if you wish. Set aside in the refrigerator.

———

Heat a large pan over a high heat. When the pan is very hot, add the mussels and water (or beer) and cover with a lid. Cook the mussels for a few minutes, or until all the shells have opened. Discard any unopened shells.

———

Drain the mussels (reserve the liquor if you like, to make a lovely sauce for another fish dish) and leave them to cool. Once cool enough to handle, pick all the meat out and reserve it.

———

To make the batter, whisk the egg white to fairly stiff peaks. In another bowl, gradually whisk the beer into the flour to form a smooth batter. Fold in the egg whites and nigella seeds, and season with a little fine salt.

———

Heat the oil in a deep-fat fryer to 180°C (350°F). Alternatively, place a deep frying pan over a high heat and add a 2cm (¾in) depth of sunflower oil. When it is hot enough, a small cube of bread added to the oil should sizzle immediately.

———

Dust the mussels in the plain flour, then place in the batter. (You can thread the mussels on skewers to make them a little easier to cook, if you like.) Using a slotted spoon, lift them out one at a time and lower them carefully into the hot oil. Fry for about 1 minute, or until golden brown all over. Remove and drain on kitchen paper, and season with fine salt.

———

To serve, spoon some tarama onto a plate and place a few mussels on top. Drizzle with mint oil and sprinkle over the spring onion.

SERVES 2–4

500g (1lb 2oz) mussels, cleaned and de-bearded

plain flour, for dusting

about 3 tablespoons water or beer

sunflower oil, for frying

1 quantity Mint Oil (see page 154), for drizzling

2 spring onions, finely sliced on the diagonal, to garnish

FOR THE TARAMA

55g (2oz) smoked cod's roe, soaked in cold water for 2 hours

½ garlic clove

freshly squeezed juice of 1 lemon

½ slice white bread, crusts removed, soaked in water

2 tablespoons water

50ml (2fl oz) sunflower oil

25ml (¾fl oz) olive oil

flaky sea salt

FOR THE BATTER

1 large egg white

300ml (10fl oz) cold beer or sparkling water

175g (6oz) self-raising flour

15g (½oz) nigella seeds

fine salt

SEAFOOD VERMICELLI WITH MUSSELS, HAKE & PRAWNS

SERVES 4

12 shell-on raw tiger prawns

300ml (10fl oz) fish stock

150ml (5fl oz) extra-virgin olive oil

1 onion, diced

1 carrot, diced

2 celery sticks, diced

3 sprigs of thyme, leaves only

½ teaspoon finely grated nutmeg

1 teaspoon ground coriander

1–2 red chillies, sliced and seeds retained

1 teaspoon tomato purée

1 tablespoon sweet pepper paste (tatlı biber salçası)

4 garlic cloves, finely grated

125ml (4fl oz) red wine

100g (3½fl oz) tomato passata

200g (7oz) vermicelli, broken into small pieces

500g (1lb 2oz) mussels, cleaned and de-bearded

300g (10½fl oz) hake fillet (or any white fish), cleaned and cut into 4cm (1½in) cubes

small bunch of flat leaf parsley, finely shredded

1 lemon, cut into wedges

flaky sea salt and freshly ground black pepper

Shredded vermicelli is called şehriye in Turkish. It is often cooked with rice for an extra nutty flavour, or in soups. Here I have made it into a complete dish, taking inspiration from the Spanish dish fideuà. You can mix and match whichever fish and shellfish you like, and even include some chicken or rabbit if you want. If you have time, do make your own fish stock – this gives depth to the dish, so it needs to be packed full of flavour.

Start by peeling the prawns: you can leave the heads on if you wish. Mix the shells with the fish stock in a pan and bring to a gentle simmer for 15 minutes. Remove from the heat and leave to infuse.

———

Heat the oil in a large pan over a medium heat, add the onion, carrot, celery and thyme and cook gently for about 20 minutes, or until very soft. Add the spices, chilli, tomato purée, sweet pepper paste and garlic and continue to cook for 5 minutes.

———

Increase the heat to high and add the red wine. Bubble to reduce by half, then add the passata and strain in the fish stock. Season with salt and pepper. Turn down to a gentle simmer and cook for 15 minutes.

———

Now stir in the vermicelli, mussels, hake and prawns. Cover with a lid and cook for about 5 minutes, or until the vermicelli is soft, the mussels have opened (discard any that haven't), the prawns have turned pink and the hake is opaque. Taste to check the seasoning, sprinkle over the parsley and serve with lemon wedges.

CUTTLEFISH WITH BAHARAT, PEAS & SAMPHIRE

Just after finishing college, a few of my friends and I went to Spain for a celebratory trip to visit a friend whose family own a campsite. One evening, my friend's mum cooked us a selection of dishes, including *sepia*, or cuttlefish. At the time I had no idea what *sepia* was and she couldn't really explain it to me, but she did say that she had cooked it with peas and cinnamon. It was so yummy that I made a note of it. It wasn't until years and years later that I referred back to that notebook and, knowing more about food at this point, realized it was cuttlefish. So here is my version of that dish.

Cut open the cuttlefish and score the inside in a cross-hatch pattern. Slice it into irregular diamond shapes about 4cm (1½in) wide. Pat the cuttlefish dry with kitchen paper and keep in the refrigerator until needed.

———

Heat the measured olive oil in a small saucepan and add the onion. Cook over a medium heat until light golden brown. Remove from the heat and add the baharat.

———

Heat a large frying pan and add 1 tablespoon olive oil. Add the cuttlefish and let it fry for at least 1 minute before moving it; you want the edges to caramelize. After that, move the fish around a little in the pan and cook for 1 more minute. Now add the cooked onion, peas and samphire and cook for 1 more minute, or until the samphire has just wilted. Remove the pan from the heat, add the lemon juice, season with salt and pepper and add a little more olive oil to make a dressing in the pan. Finally, stir in the herbs and serve.

SERVES 4

2 cuttlefish with tentacles, cleaned

100ml (3½fl oz) extra-virgin olive oil, plus a little extra for frying

1 onion, diced

2 tablespoons baharat (see page 193; also available in Turkish supermarkets)

125g (4½oz) peas, fresh or frozen

100g (3½oz) samphire

freshly squeezed juice of 1 lemon

3 sprigs of mint, leaves only, thinly sliced

4 sprigs of parsley, finely chopped

flaky sea salt and freshly ground black pepper

FRIED RED MULLET, PICKLED APRICOTS & CAPER LEAVES

SERVES 4

100g (3½oz) plain flour

1 teaspoon fine salt

4 red mullet, scaled and gutted, filleted if you prefer

50g (1¾oz) capers (lightly rinsed) or caper leaves

1 onion, cut into large dice

small bunch of flat leaf parsley, leaves only

small bunch of coriander, leaves only

small bunch of purslane, roughly chopped

50ml (2fl oz) extra-virgin olive oil, plus extra for frying

2 tablespoons red wine vinegar flaky sea salt and freshly ground black pepper

FOR THE PICKLED APRICOTS

300ml (10fl oz) water

100g (3½oz) caster sugar

1 tablespoon coriander seeds, lightly toasted and crushed

150ml (5fl oz) cider vinegar

12 dried apricots, preferably natural, halved

This dish pays homage to my *nene*'s fried fish. While I was growing up, we would visit my grandparents in Cyprus every summer, and one of the first things Nene would cook is fried fish with a big bowl of salad. Dede (Grandad) would go to the nearest town to pick up a bag of mixed little fish, a trip that I reckon took almost four hours by the time he had stopped off for a coffee and put the world to rights with his friends (also bearing in mind that his favoured mode of transport was his tractor).

First make the pickled apricots: put the water in a pan with the sugar, coriander seeds and vinegar. Bring it to the boil and add the apricots. Reduce the heat to a simmer and cook gently for 5 minutes. Using a slotted spoon, lift out the apricots and set aside in a bowl. Turn the heat back up to reduce the liquid to a light syrup. Once it is the right consistency, pour it over the apricots and leave to cool.

——

Add the capers, onion, parsley, coriander, purslane, olive oil and vinegar to the cooled apricots, along with a little of their syrup. Season with salt and pepper.

——

Season the fish with the fine salt and leave for about 10 minutes. Heat 2cm (¾in) depth of oil in a large frying pan over a medium heat. Place the fish in the flour and coat well, rubbing the flour mixture thoroughly into the fish.

——

Lower the fish carefully into the hot oil and fry until the underside is golden – about 3 minutes. Turn the fish over and do the same on the other side. Drain on kitchen paper and season with a little more fine salt. Serve with a pile of the apricot salad plus an extra drizzle of the apricot syrup and olive oil.

PISTACHIO-CRUSTED COD WITH PRESERVED LEMON BUTTER SAUCE

SERVES 4

4 cod fillets (from a sustainable source), about 175g (6oz) each, skinned and pin-boned

FOR THE PISTACHIO CRUST

100g (3½oz) pistachios, shelled and toasted

15g (½oz) fresh breadcrumbs

70g (2½oz) unsalted butter, softened

FOR THE PRESERVED LEMON SAUCE

1 whole preserved lemon (see page 201)

150ml (5fl oz) double cream

75g (2¾oz) cold unsalted butter, diced

small bunch of chives, thinly sliced

Most people think of nuts as a snack, or associate them with desserts. However, I love using them in savoury recipes too, especially pistachios – the lovely nutty flavour compliments all sorts of dishes. Some of the best pistachios in the world come from Gaziantep in Turkey, so if you see them, be sure to buy a packet.

First make the pistachio crust: put all the ingredients in a food processor and blend to a coarse paste. Spread a little of the paste over each cod fillet to make a layer about 5mm (¼in) thick, then set aside in the refrigerator.

Preheat the oven to 220°C (425°F), Gas Mark 7. To make the sauce, scoop the flesh out of the preserved lemon and put the flesh in a small saucepan with the double cream. Bring to the boil, then turn down to a simmer and reduce by one-third.

Finely dice the preserved lemon skin. Once the cream has reduced, remove the pan from the heat and whisk in the butter a cube at a time. Strain through a fine sieve and add the diced lemon skin. Cover with clingfilm and keep warm until needed.

Bake the cod in the oven for 7–9 minutes, or until just firm to touch and lightly coloured on top. Stir the chives into the preserved lemon sauce and serve with the fish.

SEA BASS WITH CARAMELIZED SHALLOT PURÉE & POMEGRANATE DRESSING

Sea bass is one of the most popular fish in Turkey and Cyprus, usually served simply charcoal-grilled with a wedge of lemon. The thing I love about eating fish over there is that it is so seasonal, which not only protects the local species from being overfished but also ensures you get to eat them at their best. Other popular fish in the eastern Mediterranean are sea bream, turbot, grouper, blue fish and red mullet and can be used instead of sea bass.

Preheat the oven to 210°C (400°F fan), Gas Mark 6.

———

First make the purée: melt the butter in a medium saucepan and add the shallots. Cook over a low heat until golden brown – this can take up to 30 minutes.

———

Meanwhile, heat the oil in an ovenproof frying pan. Add the banana shallots, cut-side down. When they start to turn golden brown, put the pan in the oven and roast the shallots for about 15 minutes.

———

While the shallots for the purée are still hot, put them in a blender with the double cream and blend until smooth. Season with salt and pepper

———

To make the dressing, combine all the ingredients in a bowl and whisk together.

———

To cook the fish, heat a drizzle of oil in a non-stick frying pan over a medium-high heat. Season the sea bass, place in the pan skin-side down and cook gently until the skin is golden brown and crisp (this should take no more than a few minutes). Turn it over and cook the flesh side for 30–60 seconds, then take it out of the pan immediately so that it doesn't overcook.

———

To serve, reheat the purée and put a spoonful on each serving plate. Place the fish on top, skin-side up, and spoon over the pomegranate dressing. Add the roasted shallots. Stir the pomegranate dressing as it will have sepatated, then dot it around the plates and serve.

SERVES 4

sunflower oil, for frying

2 banana shallots, unpeeled and halved lengthways

4 sea bass fillets, about 125g (4½oz) each, scaled and pin-boned

FOR THE CARAMELIZED SHALLOT PURÉE

2 heaped tablespoons unsalted butter

6 shallots, sliced

50ml (2fl oz) double cream

fine salt and freshly ground pepper

FOR THE POMEGRANATE DRESSING

3 tablespoons pomegranate seeds

3 tablespoons pomegranate molasses

1 banana shallot, finely chopped

6 tablespoons extra-virgin olive oil

1 small garlic clove, finely grated

1 teaspoon thyme leaves

PAN-FRIED MACKEREL, BLACK OLIVE CROUTE & TOMATO-POMEGRANATE SALAD

SERVES 4

sunflower oil, for frying

4 mackerel fillets, pin-boned

1 tablespoon ground fennel

2 tablespoons Turkish chilli flakes (pul biber)

2 tablespoons black olive paste (available in Turkish supermarkets) or use tapenade instead

FOR THE CROUTES

4 white baguette slices, cut diagonally, 1cm (½in) thick

olive oil, for drizzling

flaky sea salt

FOR THE SALAD

2 tomatoes, peeled and sliced

1 red onion, thinly sliced

2 long green Turkish peppers (Charleston peppers; use ordinary peppers if you can't find them), sliced

small bunch of flat leaf parsley, finely shredded

4 tablespoons extra-virgin olive oil

2 tablespoons pomegranate molasses

freshly ground black pepper

All along the Galata Bridge in Istanbul you will find small vendors, mostly on boats, selling grilled mackerel sandwiches called *balik ekmek*. They are utterly delicious. This is my slightly pimped-up version, but instead of making the croutes you could use a good crusty baguette.

Preheat the oven to 190°C (375°F), Gas Mark 5.

———

First make the croutes. Drizzle a little olive oil on the slices of bread, sprinkle with salt and put them on a baking tray. Bake for about 10 minutes, or until lightly golden and crisp.

———

Mix the tomatoes, red onion, peppers, parsley, olive oil and pomegranate molasses with a little salt and pepper.

———

Heat a little sunflower oil in a large frying pan over a medium-high heat. Season the mackerel on the flesh side with salt, ground fennel and chilli flakes, pressing the seasoning in. Put the fish, skin-side down, in the hot frying pan and cook for about 2 minutes, or until the skin is golden and crisp. Turn it over and cook for 1 more minute, or until just cooked through.

———

To serve, spread some black olive paste over the croute, add some tomato salad and place the mackerel on top.

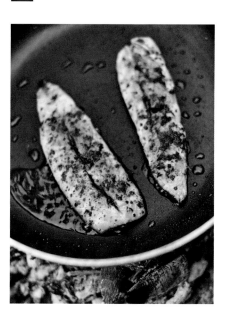

MONKFISH, CITRUS, URFA CHILLI DRESSING & CORIANDER

While I was researching food from the Byzantine era as a link between Turkey and Italy, I found a connection in the use of spices and *garum* (fish sauce). So I created a black pepper dressing, which later turned into an urfa chilli dressing. Any charcoal-grilled fish would work very well here.

Heat a barbecue until the coals turn grey. Alternatively, preheat the oven to 220°C (425°F), Gas Mark 7.

——

First make the caramel: put the sugar in a heavy-based saucepan over a high heat. Watch until it turns deep brown, carefully tilting the pan to swirl the sugar around. As soon as the caramel reaches the right colour, carefully add the orange juice, standing well back. The caramel will seize up, so keep stirring into the edge of the pan to release it. The mixture will all come together and reduce as you cook it; you want a syrupy consistency. To test this, you can drizzle a little onto a plate and place it in the refrigerator (once cooled, it should hold its own shape without running too much). Finish it with a little squeeze of lemon juice. Set aside at room temperature.

——

Whisk together all the ingredients for the urfa chilli dressing, and set aside at room temperature.

——

Pat the monkfish dry with kitchen paper. Coat it in olive oil and season with salt. Place directly on the very hot barbecue rack. Cook for 4–5 minutes, then turn it over and cook for another 4–5 minutes; you want caramelized grill marks and for the fish to feel firm to the touch. Alternatively, place the monkfish in a large roasting tray and roast in the oven for 6–8 minutes on each side. Remove from the heat, add a drizzle of olive oil and a squeeze of lemon juice, then leave to rest for 10 minutes.

——

To serve, quickly flash the monkfish on the barbecue or in the oven to reheat. Put it on a serving plate and drizzle the blood orange caramel around it. Add a good helping of urfa chilli dressing, orange segments and coriander and serve straight away.

SERVES 4

- 1 monkfish tail (about 1 kg/ 2lb 4oz), trimmed and cleaned
- 2 tablespoons olive oil
- 1 blood orange or ordinary orange, peeled and segmented
- small bunch of coriander, leaves only, but with a little stalk
- flaky or fine sea salt

FOR THE BLOOD ORANGE CARAMEL

- 50g (1¾oz) caster sugar
- 250g (9oz) blood oranges or ordinary oranges, juiced
- squeeze of lemon juice

FOR THE URFA CHILLI DRESSING

- 25g (1oz) urfa chilli flakes (isot biber)
- 50ml (2fl oz) fish sauce
- 2 tablespoons honey
- 2 tablespoons soy sauce
- 2 teaspoons ground cumin
- 2 teaspoons ground coriander
- 125ml (4fl oz) extra-virgin olive oil
- freshly squeezed juice of ½ lemon

OKLAVA AT HOME:
DINNER PARTY BY LAURA CHRISTIE

Dinner parties are the perfect excuse to have a crack at some of the more complex recipes in this book – see right for a suggested menu. Preparing these dishes may at times keep you away from your guests, but their amazed queries of 'How did you make this?' will make it all worthwhile. We recommend serving these dishes on large sharing platters in the middle of the table.

Turkish wine is the obvious accompaniment to Turkish food. My white of choice would be Paşaeli Yapincak, which spends time in oak but still retains a ripe citrus note with touches of stone fruit and orange zest. It's enjoyable alone but fantastic with food, as the complexity added by the oak gives it enough backbone to stand up to the punchy flavours of Turkish cooking.

I first came across this wine on a trip to Istanbul with Selin. On our last night, we took a slightly hairy cab ride followed by a private water taxi to reach a fish restaurant on the very edge of the Bosporus. I wanted to try the Yapincak grape (pronounced 'yap-in-jack'). The wine we drank was from a winemaker I had not previously come across but, carried away by the food and spectacular view, I forgot to make a note of the name. However, I did remember the distinctive label with its images of fish. Fast forward several weeks and I spotted the wine at a tasting in London. Accompanying it was the winemaker, Seyit, who has since become a great supporter of Oklava. Paşaeli are committed to promoting indigenous varieties, and Yapincak is native to the Şarköy area in Thrace. Minimum intervention is used in the vineyards, and organic wine methods are used as far is as practical in a modern, medium-sized winery.

A remarkable red for a dinner party is the Arcadia Cabernet Franc. Perfect with the bolder and fuller flavours of Turkish cooking, this wine will be a real surprise to any Turkish wine sceptics. The Arcadia winery was founded over ten years ago by father and daughter Zeynep and Ozcan, possibly the most welcoming hosts in Turkey. Selin and I first visited Arcadia in the summer of 2015, and it is everything I have come to love about small-scale wine production – a family affair and a project of real passion. Great care is taken to look after the land, involve the community and insist on careful production methods. The end products are amazing wines that reflect the beauty of their surroundings.

Cabernet Franc is an international grape, so the flavour profile of this wine, which includes plum, blackcurrant and liquorice, and aromas like tobacco (from the year spent in French oak) will be familiar to many. Full-bodied with elegant tannins, it benefits from being decanted – or simply pour the wine into glasses and enjoy an aperitif while giving it a few minutes to open up.

DINNER PARTY MENU: FOR 6–8 PEOPLE

BAHARAT-SPICED BREAD WITH MEDJOOL DATE BUTTER (PAGES 46 & 186)

SOUR CHERRY PEARL BARLEY, CRISPY KALE, YOGURT, CHILLI BUTTER & SHEEP'S CHEESE (PAGE 157)

ROMAINE LETTUCE SALAD WITH CANDIED WALNUTS & FETA DRESSING (PAGE 18)

CHILLI-ROAST CAULIFLOWER (PAGE 136)

RICOTTA DUMPLINGS WITH YOGURT SAUCE, CHILLI BUTTER & PINE NUTS (PAGE 154)

SEA BASS WITH CARAMELIZED SHALLOT PURÉE & POMEGRANATE DRESSING (PAGE 126)

ÇEMEN-BRAISED SHORT RIBS WITH BROWN BUTTER BREAD SAUCE (PAGE 86)

CRISPY POMEGRANATE-GLAZED LAMB BREAST WITH YOGURT (PAGE 96)

SPICED RICE PUDDING BRÛLÉE, PISTACHIOS, CARAMELIZED PINEAPPLE, RUM JELLY, LYCHEES & LIME (PAGE 207)

TURKISH COFFEE (PAGE 172)

OKLAVA AT HOME:
DATE NIGHT BY LAURA CHRISTIE

For date night, keep things simple but impressive. Our Cypriot 75 (see page 180) makes an elegant start to any special evening: it is very simple to make if you have a lot of cooking to do, and the flavours are neither too sweet nor too bitter. It's also easy to top up if you decide to stick to the cocktail through the meal.

A favourite wine for date nights at the restaurant is Kalecik Karası, pronounced 'kah-le-jik car-ah-su' (or KK, as we call it for short). Among the things we love about Turkish wines are the names of the grapes, and this one means 'black from the small castle'. Kalecik is a small village with a castle north-east of Ankara in Central Anatolia, and it's the home of this grape variety. Also located near Ankara is the producer of this wine, Vinkara, a sophisticated and modern winery with a passion for indigenous varieties. Most of Turkish wine that makes it to export comes from the Aegean region, so getting some inland examples on the list has been fantastic.

Kalecik Karası typifies exactly what I want to serve at Oklava: wines that are recognizable to the palate but have their own unique twist. The slightly gamey and savoury notes against a background of redcurrant and sweet spice in this light red remind me of a Gamay or Pinot Noir, but the red-rose colour and slight candy on the nose are classically Turkish, making this an interesting and complex wine, perfect for a romantic evening in.

CHILLI-ROAST CAULIFLOWER

I created this dish after my first visit to Istanbul. I had brought back with me a hot sun-dried pepper paste and some pistachios from one of the incredible markets out there. At home one evening, I had a cauliflower, some parsley and the pepper paste in my fridge – and so the chilli-roast cauliflower was born. I cooked it at my very first pop-up, where it became an instant hit, and it is now our top seller at Oklava.

Preheat the oven to 210°C (400°F), Gas Mark 6 and line a baking tray with baking parchment. Cut the cauliflower into 4–6 even wedges depending on its size, keeping a little of the stalk on to hold the wedges. Rinse under cold water and pat dry with kitchen paper.

———

Mix the two pepper pastes with the olive oil and a little salt. Rub the mixture all over the cauliflower wedges (you might want to wear gloves to do this) and put them on the prepared baking tray. Bake for 10–13 minutes, or until just tender. I like to make sure the cauliflower still has a good bite to it. Set aside.

———

Drain the red onions, pat dry with kitchen paper and set aside.

———

Heat a dry non-stick frying pan on the hob. Once hot, add the cauliflower wedges and cook for a minute or so on each side, or until slightly charred.

———

To serve, put the wedges on a large plate and top with the parsley, red onion and pistachios. Drizzle with plenty of the sumac dressing and an extra sprinkling of sumac before serving.

SERVES 4–6

1 cauliflower (keep the green leaves on if they are nice)

2 heaped tablespoons Turkish hot pepper paste (açi biber salçasi)

4 heaped tablespoons Turkish sweet pepper paste (tatli biber salçasi)

50ml (2fl oz) extra-virgin olive oil

1 large handful flat leaf parsley leaves

½ red onion, sliced as thinly as possible and soaked in ice water

5 tablespoons pistachio nuts, toasted and roughly chopped

1 quantity Sumac Dressing (see page 194)

1 teaspoon sumac

flaky sea salt

SPICY RED LENTIL KÖFTES WITH LETTUCE, SPRING ONIONS & LEMON

We sometimes had these as a tasty light meal on a hot summer day when I was growing up. They can also be made with raw minced lamb instead of red lentils; that version is called *cig köfte*. **Expert makers knead these for ages by hand, and street vendors all around Turkey used to sell raw lamb** *köfte*, **ready to be cooked at home. These lentil** *köftes* **are great for any time of the week, even Sunday brunch.**

Heat the olive oil in a pan over a medium heat, add the onions and cook for about 10 minutes, or until tender and translucent. Add the cumin, paprika and hot pepper paste and cook for 1 more minute. Add the lentils and stir well. Cover with enough cold water to reach 2cm (¾in) above the lentils. Bring to the boil, reduce the heat to low and cook for about 20 minutes, or until nearly all the water has evaporated and the lentils are cooked through. You might need to add a little more water. Turn the heat off and add the bulgur wheat. Stir well, cover the pan with clingfilm and leave to stand for 30 minutes. Slice 3 of the spring onions diagonally and place them in iced water.

———

Remove the clingfilm from the lentil mixture and transfer to a large bowl. Let it cool a little before seasoning with salt. Finely slice the remaining spring onions and add to the lentils along with the chopped parsley. Knead the mixture well for 10 minutes, or put it in a stand mixer and beat with the paddle attachment until the mixture forms a ball.

———

Now divide the mixture into 25–30 equal size pieces and shape into sausages or balls, depending on how big you would like them to be. Arrange the lettuce leaves on a serving platter with the sliced spring onions, the sprigs of parsley and the lemon wedges. To eat them, take a lettuce leaf and place a köfte inside, then top with spring onions, parsley and a good squeeze of lemon.

MAKES 25–30

200ml (7fl oz) extra-virgin olive oil

2 onions, finely chopped

1 heaped teaspoon ground cumin

1 heaped teaspoon sweet smoked paprika

2 tablespoons hot pepper paste (açi biber salçasi)

450g (1lb) red lentils, rinsed with cold water

275g (9¾oz) fine bulgur wheat

1½ bunches of spring onions, thinly sliced

bunch of flat leaf parsley, finely chopped (a little stalk it good), plus extra sprigs to serve

1 head of Romaine lettuce

2 lemons, cut into wedges

fine salt

SPICED CHICKPEAS, BUTTERED CABBAGE, POACHED DUCK EGG & TULUM CHEESE

This dish is perfect for lunch, or even brunch. Chickpeas take on all sorts of flavours and lots of spice really well, so if you like things hot, add more urfa chilli. For some extra texture you could add Çemen Crumbs too (see page 39).

Heat the olive oil in a pan over a medium heat, add the onion and cook gently for about 10 minutes, or until completely soft. Add the garlic, spices and tomato purée and continue to cook for a few minutes. Now add the chickpeas and red wine. Increase the heat to reduce the wine by half, then add about 3 tablespoons water and season with salt and pepper. Turn the heat right down and cook gently for 10 minutes.

———

Meanwhile, bring a small pan of water to the boil, add the vinegar and lower the heat to a simmer. Crack the duck eggs into the water, then cook them to your liking; if you prefer them soft, you just want to set the white and the yolk should be soft when you touch it. (If you want to get ahead, you can poach the eggs, then transfer them to iced water until needed. To serve, gently reheat them in a pan of water.)

———

While the eggs are cooking, melt the butter in a pan, add the cabbage leaves with a splash of water, cover and cook for 2–3 minutes, or until wilted. Season with salt and pepper.

———

Stir some of the parsley through the chickpeas and divide them between 2 serving bowls. Scatter over the cabbage and top each serving with an egg. Scatter over the cheese and a little more parsley to serve.

SERVES 2

100ml (3½fl oz) extra-virgin olive oil

1 onion, chopped

3 garlic cloves, finely grated

1 heaped teaspoon sweet smoked paprika

1 teaspoon ground fennel

2 tablespoons urfa chilli flakes (isot biber)

1 tablespoon tomato purée

400g (14oz) tinned chickpeas, drained and rinsed

125ml (4fl oz) red wine

2 tablespoons white vinegar

2 duck eggs, the freshest you can find

small bunch of flat leaf parsley, chopped (a little stalk is good)

1 teaspoon unsalted butter

¼ head of sweetheart cabbage, cored and leaves separated

4 tablespoons tulum cheese or any strong, crumbly cheese

flaky sea salt and freshly ground black pepper

SLOW-COOKED WHITE BEANS WITH TOMATO, LEMON & OLIVE OIL

SERVES 6–8

250ml (9fl oz) extra-virgin olive oil

2 carrots, diced

2 celery sticks, diced

2 onions, diced

1 bay leaf

2 sprigs of thyme, leaves only

3 garlic cloves, thinly sliced

400g (14oz) dried white beans, such as cannellini, soaked overnight

½ head of cabbage, such as sweetheart, finely shredded

3-4 large tomatoes, peeled and roughly diced

small bunch of flat leaf parsley, chopped (a little stalk is good)

1 sprig of tarragon, leaves only

1 sprig of marjoram or oregano, leaves only, chopped

finely grated zest of 1 lemon

flaky sea salt and freshly ground black pepper

The Turks love their beans and have all sorts of recipes for the different types, sometimes with meat and sometimes without. The key to this dish, traditionally made with a rich tomato sauce known as *kuru fasulye*, is to use the best ingredients you can get hold of, as the flavours are very subtle. It is traditionally served with raw onion, bread and parsley to mop up all the juices, a great mid-week meal. I especially like to cook this version in the summer months, as it tastes a little lighter and fresher because of the lemon zest.

Heat the oil in a large pan over a low heat. Add the carrots, celery, onions, bay leaf and thyme. Cover and cook gently for about 15 minutes, or until slightly softened. Add the garlic and continue to cook for 5 minutes.

——

Drain the beans, add to the pan and pour in enough water to cover them by 5cm (2in). Gently cook for about 30 minutes, or until the beans are almost soft. You might need to add a bit more water if the pan starts to dry out.

——

Add the cabbage and tomatoes (there should be enough liquid to come halfway up the beans at this point; if there is too much, just spoon some out). Season with salt and pepper, cover and cook for 5 minutes, or until the cabbage has wilted but still has a little bite.

——

Remove from the heat, check the seasoning and add the parsley, tarragon and marjoram. Serve in bowls and scatter over the lemon zest; a little extra olive oil, flaky sea salt and parsley on top are always good too.

BARBECUED SWEETCORN WITH SUMAC, GARLIC, LEMON BUTTER & ZA'ATAR

In Cyprus people will set up a small barbecue just about anywhere, and you'll often see them selling freshly grilled corn cobs in their husks. When I'm having a barbecue at home, I nearly always grill corn as one of the courses. I just love it, especially experimenting with all the different flavours it can take. I like to open up the cupboards and see what jumps out at me.

Heat a barbecue until the coals turn grey. Place the corn cobs straight onto the rack and leave to blister and blacken slightly, turning them over.

———

Meanwhile, combine the butter, sumac, lemon, garlic and salt in a bowl and mix well. You can make the butter ahead of time, if you like: just place it on a piece of cling film, roll it into a sausage shape and keep refrigerated until needed.

———

Once the corn is cooked to your liking, remove it from the grill, leave to cool just a little and peel back the husks. Smear over the butter and sprinkle with za'atar. Garnish with coriander and serve with wedges of lime.

SERVES 4

4 corn cobs, with husks
4 tablespoons unsalted butter, softened
1 tablespoon sumac
finely grated zest of 1 lemon
2 garlic cloves, finely grated
1 teaspoon flaky sea salt
2 tablespoons za'atar
1 lime, cut into wedges
4 sprigs of coriander, mostly leaves with a little stalk

BAKED LAMB-FAT POTATOES, FRIED DUCK EGG, GRILLED HELLIM & SHERRY VINEGAR CARAMEL

As a quick and easy dinner, Mum would sometimes sauté a pile of diced potatoes, then crack an egg onto it, or add some diced lamb with caramelized onion and parsley. It was one of my favourite meals. This is my rather more complex version of that dish, which captures the flavours of a good lamb roast with potatoes. Leftover fat from a lamb roast is perfect here, or ask your butcher for lamb suet.

If using lamb suet, place it in a pan over a low heat, cook gently to draw out the fat, then strain through a sieve before using. Heat half the lamb fat or suet in a large pan over a medium heat. Add the lamb breast, onions and both types of peppers and cook for 45–60 minutes, or until completely softened. Season with fine salt. Once cooked, drain the lamb, adding the fat to the remaining lamb fat or suet and keep it warm.

Preheat the oven to 190°C (375°F), Gas Mark 5 and line a deep baking tray (about 20 x 30/8 x 12in) with baking parchment. Cut the potatoes into 2–3mm (¹/₁₆–¹/₈in) slices, using a mandoline if you have one. Coat the slices in the lamb fat in a heatproof bowl. If they get stuck together, hold the bowl over a low heat or place briefly in the oven to melt the fat again.

Place 3 layers of potatoes in the bottom of the prepared tray, overlapping them a little and seasoning with salt. Add a thin layer of the lamb mixture, followed by another 2 layers of potatoes and seasoning. Keep repeating this process until all the potatoes and lamb mixture are used up. Try to finish with 3 layers of potatoes on the top. Reserve any leftover fat.

Put a sheet of baking parchment directly on top of the potatoes and push them down so they are evenly spread out in the tray and into the corners. Cover with foil and bake for about 45–60 minutes, until the potatoes are soft (check by poking a skewer or knife into the centre).

Once cooked, remove from the oven and leave to rest for 40 minutes. Place another tray and a weight on top to press it down, then chill the gratin for at least 3 hours, or overnight.

Preheat the oven to 200°C (400°F), Gas Mark 6. To release the gratin, you'll need to warm the tray, either by using a blowtorch or running it across a low heat. Turn it out and cut into 12 portions. Heat a frying pan with a little more lamb fat (or sunflower oil) and add the portions of gratin. Cook until crispy and golden on both sides. Transfer to a baking tray and put in the oven for 5 minutes to heat through.

Meanwhile, fry the duck eggs in more lamb fat or sunflower oil. In a separate frying pan, fry the slices of hellim in a little sunflower oil until golden brown on both sides. Serve the eggs on top of the hot gratin with a drizzle of sherry vinegar caramel, a slice of hellim and a few parsley leaves to garnish.

SERVES 12

200–300g (7–10½oz) lamb fat or lamb suet, melted

250g (9oz) lamb breast, sliced into small pieces

1–2 onions, chopped

4 long green Turkish peppers (Charleston peppers; use ordinary peppers if you can't find them), sliced

4 hot Turkish peppers (sivri biber; use any hot chillies if you can't find them)

8 large white potatoes (we like to use the variety Cyprus)

12 duck eggs

1 x 250g (9oz) block hellim (halloumi), sliced into 6

1 quantity Sherry Vinegar Caramel (see page 195)

fine salt

flat leaf parsley leaves, to garnish

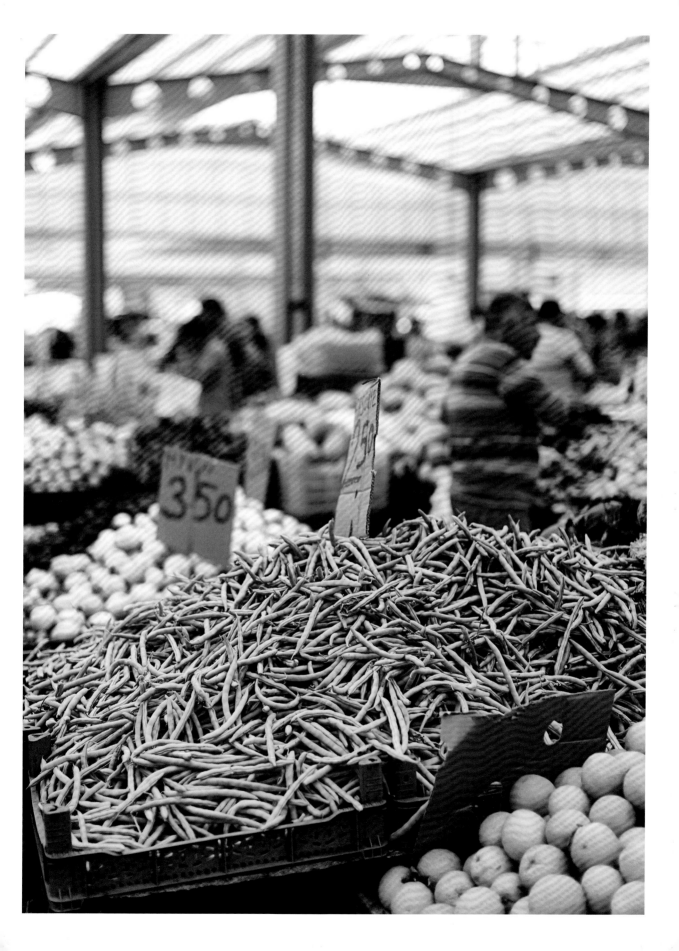

CRISPY FRIED SPRING ONIONS, CHEESE SAUCE & ÇEMEN CRUMBS

A few years ago I discovered *calçots*, the delicious spring onions from Catalonia in Spain. I tried preparing them in the traditional way, which is to blacken them, peel off the outer layer and eat them with romesco sauce. As delicious as this was, I had an urge to fry them in spiced flour. This is a great, indulgent dish by itself, or you could serve it as a garnish with grilled steak, or even top a *pide* with them. If you can find *calçots*, I would recommend using them.

Mix the flour with the spices and measured salt, and set aside.

—

Slice the onions diagonally into 1cm (½in) slices. Whisk the milk and yogurt together in a bowl. Add the onions and leave to soak for about 30 minutes.

—

Heat the oil in a deep-fat fryer to 180°C (350°F). Alternatively, half fill a deep frying pan with oil and set over a high heat. When hot enough, a small cube of bread added to the oil should sizzle immediately.

—

Take a handful of the onions, shake off the excess milk mixture and coat them in the flour. Transfer to a sieve and shake off the excess flour, then add them carefully to the hot oil and fry for about 2 minutes, or until golden brown. Remove and drain on kitchen paper to soak up the excess oil and season with fine salt.

—

To serve, put the cheese sauce in a large bowl or several smaller bowls and top with a mound of fried onions and a generous sprinkling of çemen crumbs.

SERVES 4–6

200g (7oz) plain flour

1 heaped tablespoon sweet smoked paprika

1 heaped tablespoon ground coriander

1 heaped tablespoon ground cumin

1 heaped tablespoon ground fennel

1 tablespoon fine salt, plus extra to season

2 bunches of spring onions or calçots, outer layers removed

300ml (10fl oz) milk

100ml (3½fl oz) Turkish or Greek yogurt

sunflower oil, for frying

1 quantity Cheese Sauce (see pages 56 and 65)

1 quantity Çemen Crumbs (see page 39)

SPICED RICE, APRICOT, ALMOND & FILO PIE

SERVES 6

150g (5½oz) unsalted butter

50ml (2fl oz) extra-virgin olive oil

1 onion, diced

3 garlic cloves, finely grated

1 teaspoon ground cumin

1 tablespoon fennel seeds, toasted and ground

1 tablespoon ground coriander

1 teaspoon freshly grated nutmeg

185g (6½oz) long-grain rice, rinsed

85g (3oz) dried apricots (preferably natural), diced

100g (3½oz) whole blanched almonds, toasted and roughly chopped

350ml (12fl oz) boiling water

2 large sheets of yufka, or 6 sheets filo pastry

flaky sea salt and freshly ground black pepper

Known as *perde pilav* in Turkish, this is a very traditional recipe, for which people would usually make their own dough and roll it out very thinly. Here I have tried to make it a little easier by using filo pastry (or the Turkish version, *yufka*, if you can find it, which is available in most Turkish supermarkets.) If you like, you can use different spices, nuts and fruit than those listed, and even mix in a little shredded chicken or duck.

Melt 100g (3½oz) of the butter with the olive oil in a large pan over a medium heat. Add the onion and cook gently for 10 minutes, or until golden. Add the garlic and all the spices and continue to cook for 5 minutes over a low heat. Now add the rice and season with salt and pepper, stirring to ensure it is well coated. Add the apricots, almonds and boiling water. Bring to the boil, then turn the heat down to its lowest setting, cover and cook for 20 minutes, or until all the water has evaporated and the rice is cooked.

Remove the rice from the pan and spread it out on a tray to cool down completely. Preheat the oven to 220°C (425°F), Gas Mark 7.

Melt the remaining butter and use some of it to lightly grease a 20cm (8in) round cake tin. If using yufka, drape the first sheet over the tin and press it down into the bottom and sides, allowing the excess to hang over the edge. Fill the tin with the rice mixture, pressing it out firmly and evenly. Fold the overhanging pastry over the filling and brush it with a little butter. Trim the second sheet so that it is just a little bigger than the tin. Place it on the top of the rice and, using a spoon, tuck in all the corners neatly. Brush the top with butter. If using filo, follow the same procedure, using 3 sheets to line the tin and 3 trimmed sheets on top, brushing each sheet with butter.

———

Bake for about 25 minutes, or until golden brown and crisp. Remove the pie from the oven and leave to rest for 5 minutes. Carefully turn it onto a plate and leave to rest for another 10 minutes. Slice into 6 portions to serve.

VEGETABLE DOLMAS

These are called *yalanci dolma* in Turkish: dolma refers to anything stuffed, and *yalanci* means 'liar', as this version does not contain the usual meat. Mum is a complete pro at any sort of dolma, and is known in our circle for making the best. Throughout the summer she makes them using vine leaves, which she grows herself in the garden, and in the winter she moves on to different types of cabbage. This version, using cabbage leaves, is a good place to start, and once you have mastered it, you can move onto vine leaves, which are a little fiddlier to handle. You could also use the Artichoke Dolma filling (see page 84) to stuff cabbage or vine leaves.

SERVES 8–10

2 whole Savoy or green cabbages, stalk removed

500g (1lb 2oz) white long-grain rice, rinsed

2 onions, finely chopped

400g (14oz) tinned plum tomatoes, chopped

2 tablespoons dried mint

125ml (4fl oz) extra-virgin olive oil

freshly squeezed juice of 2–3 lemons (we like our dolmas with a zing; use 2 if you don't)

flaky sea salt and freshly ground black pepper

Bring a large pan of water to the boil. Separate the cabbage leaves, making sure you keep them intact. As long as the leaf is big enough to roll into a cigar shape, it is usable.

———

In a large bowl, mix together the rice, onions, tomatoes, mint, oil and lemon juice, then season with salt and pepper. Set aside.

———

Blanch the cabbage leaves in batches of 5 for about 1 minute, until they are just pliable. Remove and place on a large tray to cool.

———

To make the dolmas, take a large cabbage leaf and place a heaped tablespoon of the rice mixture in a line across the stalk end, as in the photo opposite. Do not go right to the edges. Working from the edge closest to you, roll up the leaf tightly to form a cigar shape. The sides will roll in naturally. Put the dolma in a large, wide-based pan with a lid.

———

Repeat the process until all the leaves are used up or you run out of mixture. As the leaves get smaller you will need less stuffing. It is very important to pack the dolmas in tight layers in the pan. It's fine to put them on top of one another, but do not go right to the top of the pan, as you need to leave room for them to expand. Boil the kettle and pour over just enough hot water to cover the top layer of dolmas. Put an upside-down plate directly on top of the dolmas to hold them down. Set the pan over a high heat; as soon as the water comes to the boil, reduce the heat to medium-low, put the lid on and cook for 40–45 minutes, or until all the water has evaporated.

———

Once cooked, take the pan off the heat and remove the plate. Put a couple of pieces of kitchen paper on top of the dolmas and put the lid back on. Leave to stand for about 15–20 minutes before serving; I like them best served at room temperature.

RICOTTA DUMPLINGS WITH YOGURT SAUCE, CHILLI BUTTER & PINE NUTS

These small pasta dumplings are called *pirohu* **in Cyprus and** *manti* **in Turkey. My version takes a little time, but I believe it's totally worth the effort.**

First make the dumpling dough: mix the flour and salt in a bowl. Keep mixing while you slowly pour in the water until a dough forms. Tip it onto a floured surface and knead for about 5 minutes, or until smooth. Cover with clingfilm and rest in the refrigerator for at least 1 hour.

To make the mint oil, put the dried mint and olive oil in a small pan and heat gently for 5 minutes. Set aside to infuse.

To make the sauce, heat the olive oil in a pan, add the shallots and cook gently until golden brown. Add the garlic and thyme and cook for a further few minutes. Now add the wine and simmer to reduce by half, then add the cream and reduce by one-third. Remove from the heat and whisk in the yogurt. Using a stick blender, blend the sauce until smooth and season with salt. Leave to cool and set aside in the refrigerator.

Preheat the oven to 210°C (400°F), Gas Mark 6. Put the cabbage wedges on a baking tray, drizzle with a little olive oil and season with salt. Bake for about 15 minutes, or until the edges are a little charred and the cabbage is tender but not overcooked. Set aside. Turn the oven down to 180°C (350°F), Gas Mark 4.

Combine the ingredients for the filling and season to taste. Set aside.

To make the dumplings, cut the dough in half and cover 1 piece with a damp tea towel. Roll the other into a circle 2–3mm ($^1/_{16}$–$^1/_8$in) thick.

Place about 18 teaspoons of the ricotta mixture on one half of the pastry sheet, spaced evenly apart. Brush the other half of the circle lightly with water if it seems to be too dry to stick by itself. Fold over the circle and push down to seal the edges neatly around each pile of ricotta. Cut out each dumpling using a cup or pastry cutter. Place on a tray or plate heavily dusted with semolina. Repeat with the remaining dough and filling.

Bring a large pan of salted water to the boil. Melt the chilli butter and keep it warm. Cut the stalks out of the cabbage quarters and put them in the oven to reheat. Gently reheat the yogurt sauce until it is just warm to the touch, then cover with a lid.

Working in batches, put the dumplings in the boiling water for 1–2 minutes. Transfer to a bowl with some of the cooking water to stop them sticking while you cook the rest. To serve, divide the cabbage and dumplings between 4 plates. Spoon over the warm yogurt sauce. Drizzle over some chilli butter and mint oil. Finally, scatter over the pine nuts and thyme leaves.

MAKES ABOUT 36

1 sweetheart cabbage, cut into 4 wedges

extra-virgin olive oil, for drizzling

semolina, for dusting

½ quantity Chilli Butter (see page 186)

50g (1¾oz) pine nuts, lightly toasted

1 tablespoon thyme leaves

flaky fine salt

FOR THE DOUGH

250g (9oz) plain flour

½ teaspoon fine salt

200–300ml (7–10fl oz) cold water

FOR THE MINT OIL

1 teaspoon dried mint

4 tablespoons extra-virgin olive oil

FOR THE SAUCE

50ml (2fl oz) extra-virgin olive oil

3 banana shallots, chopped

3 garlic cloves, finely grated

1 sprig of thyme, leaves only

125ml (4fl oz) white wine

500ml (18fl oz) double cream

400ml (14fl oz) Turkish or Greek yogurt

FOR THE FILLING

500g (1lb 2oz) ricotta cheese

small bunch of flat leaf parsley, leaves only, chopped

small bunch of tarragon, leaves only, chopped

8 basil leaves, chopped

freshly ground black pepper

SOUR CHERRY PEARL BARLEY, CRISPY KALE, YOGURT, CHILLI BUTTER & SHEEP'S CHEESE

SERVES 6–8

1 quantity Chilli Butter (see page 186)

6 tablespoons Turkish or Greek yoghurt

small bunch of mint, leaves only, shredded

small bunch of flat leaf parsley, leaves only, shredded

1 quantity Crispy Kale (see page 21)

60g (2¼oz) hard sheep's cheese, such as pecorino

FOR THE PEARL BARLEY

150ml (5fl oz) extra-virgin olive oil

6 banana shallots, thinly sliced

4 garlic cloves, thinly sliced

200g (7oz) dried sour cherries

250g (9oz) pearl barley, rinsed with cold water

fine salt

I'm not sure how I came up with this dish, but I'm really glad I did. It's a big crowd pleaser, which I think is because it is quite unusual and you wouldn't expect pearl barley to be so full of flavour. It found its way onto the Oklava menu after a critic wrote a review of my residency at Carousel, describing it as a highlight of her year.

First prepare the pearl barley: heat the olive oil in a pan over a very low heat, add the shallots and cook very gently for 20 minutes, until soft but with no colour. Add the garlic and continue to cook for 5 minutes. Add the sour cherries and pearl barley and stir to coat in the oil and shallots. Pour enough cold water into the pan to cover the barley by about 2cm (¾in). Gently cook over a medium heat for about 30 minutes, or until just cooked through. Season with fine salt. Meanwhile, melt the chilli butter and keep warm.

Transfer the pearl barley mixture to a serving platter or individual plates. Put the yogurt in a squeezy bottle (if you have one) and drizzle it over the top. Add the herbs and a trickle of warm chilli butter, top with the crispy kale and finely grate over the cheese.

BUTTERED FREEKEH WITH CHICKPEAS, GREEN OLIVES, CURRANTS & PISTACHIOS

SERVES 2–4

125g (4½oz) unsalted butter

50ml (2fl oz) extra-virgin olive oil

3 banana shallots, diced

3 garlic cloves, finely grated

250g (9oz) freekeh, rinsed under cold water

125g (4½oz) currants

200g (7oz) good-quality green olives, pitted and roughly chopped

700ml (1¼ pints) water

400g (14oz) tinned chickpeas, drained and rinsed

150g (5½oz) pistachios, shelled, toasted and coarsely ground

small bunch of flat leaf parsley, chopped

small bunch of mint, leaves only, shredded

small bunch of chives, chopped

flaky sea salt and freshly ground black pepper

Freekeh is a brilliantly versatile grain with a rich, slightly smoky flavour that comes from roasting over an open fire. This is a great dish by itself, as part of a sharing meze-style meal, or as an accompaniment to roasted meats or fish. We sometimes serve it with fried prawns and a wedge of lemon.

Heat the butter and olive oil in a medium pan over a medium heat. Add the shallots and cook gently for about 10 minutes, or until browned. Add the garlic and continue to cook for 2–3 minutes.

Now add the freekeh, currants and olives and season with salt and pepper. Pour in the water, reduce the heat to low and cover with a lid. Cook for about 30 minutes, stirring occasionally. Add a little extra water if it seems a bit dry. The freekeh should be just tender, but still with a little bite to it. Finally, add the chickpeas, pistachios and herbs, check the seasoning and serve.

OKLAVA AT HOME:
PERFECT PARTY FOOD BY LAURA CHRISTIE

At Oklava we believe that all special occasions should start with a glass of fizz. Our favourite is Kavaklidere Altın Köpük (literally 'golden foam'), a fantastic wine from Turkey's oldest and probably best-known winery. The indigenous grape used is Emir, which means 'lord', a name said to derive from the fact that Emir wines have occupied a place on the dinner tables of nobility as far back as Roman times.

Perfect as an aperitif, Altın Köpük is most easily comparable to Prosecco, and will be familiar in taste: predominantly green apple and white flower with a slight brioche note. This brioche note and a slight added complexity are due to the wine spending some time ageing in contact with yeast. For this reason, it is a very interesting halfway house, production-wise, between Prosecco and wines made by the Champagne method.

For a Turkish take on the classic Bellini, mix Altın Köpük with a basic fruit purée or syrup – our favourites are bergamot, pomegranate and rose. We recommend about 25ml (¾fl oz) purée or syrup, depending on concentration, to 125ml (4fl oz) wine. This is great option for a large group: you can pour the syrup or purée into glasses beforehand, ready to top up with fizz just before serving. If you can't find Altın Köpük, any Prosecco-style sparkling wine will match well with these syrups or purées, and pair perfectly with Turkish flavours.

For a cocktail option, our Pomegranate & Sumac Martini (see page 176) is a great choice, as all the work can be done in advance and the mixture refrigerated until required. You could even skip the shaking-with-ice stage and add the lime to the prepared mixture for a speedy service, although shaking cocktails in front of guests is always a nice touch. If serving this drink pre-mixed, we recommend chilling the glasses in the freezer or with ice and water first.

The dishes listed on the right are perfect to be laid out buffet-style, or even passed around, leaving you to enjoy your evening without being tied to the stove.

PARTY MENU

FRIED BEEF KÖFTE
WITH TOMATO RELISH
(PAGES 89 & 189)

CUTTLEFISH WITH
BAHARAT, PEAS &
SAMPHIRE (PAGE 120)

TOMATO, RAW ONION,
PURSLANE, CRISP
BREAD & MINT SALAD
(PAGE 15)

SALAD OF RUNNER BEANS,
CUCUMBER, FENNEL &
KALE WITH A TOMATO
DRESSING (PAGE 21)

FRIED VEGETABLES
WITH GARLIC YOGURT &
POMEGRANATE (PAGE 23)

VEGETABLE DOLMAS
(PAGE 152)

SPICED BEEF & CHEESE
SAUCE POĞAÇAS
(PAGE 56)

SEMOLINA CUSTARD &
FILO BÖREKS (PAGE 204)

HOMEMADE LIMONATA

As one famous food critic asked me in our opening weeks: is this just posh lemonade? The answer is essentially yes. All over Istanbul you see street vendors selling fresh limonata, which is extremely refreshing and easy to make and store. It's a great addition to a barbecue or for any non-drinkers. Modifications to personal taste can easily be made with the addition of almost any other fruit. The amount of sugar can also be adjusted to taste.

Bring the sugar and water to a simmer in a saucepan and heat for about 5 minutes, or until the sugar dissolves and the mixture starts to thicken. Remove from the heat and allow to cool. Mix the sugar syrup with the lemon juice and store in the refrigerator until required.

——

To serve, fill a glass with ice and add 25ml (¾in) of the lemon mixture; top up with still or sparkling water and serve with a slice of lemon or sprig of mint.

MAKES 1 LITRE

500g (1lb 2oz) granulated sugar

500ml (18fl oz) water

500ml (18fl oz) freshly squeezed lemon juice

lemon slices or mint sprigs, to serve

POMEGRANATE ICED TEA

We have always felt that it's a shame to have an interesting food and wine list but a dull soft drinks selection – an opinion Laura became more firm about on finding out she was expecting a baby a few months after Oklava opened. Pomegranate iced tea is very refreshing and simple to make, but has enough wow factor to impress guests. This recipe makes a big pitcher for sharing, but you could easily bottle and store it in the refrigerator for up to five days. It's easy to adapt the recipe – with green tea, for example, or any other kind of fruit.

Stir the sugar into the tea until dissolved, then stir in the pomegranate juice. Refrigerate until required.

——

To serve, fill the glasses with ice and pomegranate seeds, pour in the tea mixture and serve immediately.

SERVES 6

25g (1oz) granulated sugar

200ml (7fl oz) light English breakfast tea, brewed for 1 minute

600ml (20fl oz) pomegranate juice

pomegranate seeds

TRADITIONAL TURKISH ÇAY

Tea or *çay* (pronounced 'chai') is deeply embedded in Turkish culture, and is an important element of hospitality. The Turkish element is the method used to brew the tea rather than its origin, although a huge amount of tea is produced domestically in Turkey. After the First World War and the fall of the Ottoman Empire, importing coffee became hugely expensive, so the popularity of tea exploded. You will see it served everywhere in the traditional tulip-shaped glasses that have become as quintessentially Turkish as the red phone box is British.

Tea is served without milk from a special teapot called a *çaydanlık*. This looks like two teapots stacked on top of each other: the bottom one is larger and is used to boil water, while the upper one is used to brew a very strong tea. Each serving of tea is then made by diluting liquid from the upper pot using water from the bottom pot according to the drinker's individual taste, and it is frequently served with sugar. As the tea is consumed, the upper pot is topped up with water from the bottom pot, and new water is added to the bottom pot to keep the tea going for several hours. Tea is drunk all year round and at every time of day – even during the very hot summers, when it is said to help cool you down. We were offered many glasses during our time in the markets of Istanbul as a friendly refresher during price negotiations, and it is also extremely popular served at home to welcome guests.

We use Özerlat tea in the restaurant, but any good Turkish supermarket will stock tea, or it is easily available online. If you are planning to be a regular drinker, electric *çaydanlıks* are easily available online and well worth the investment. If the tea is to be served with brunch, I would suggest using an ordinary teapot and a kettle. Use loose-leaf tea to brew a pot of strong tea for about 10 minutes, then pour it into glasses (or cups) and top up with hot water from the kettle. The colour should be an amber-toffee tone, but try it beforehand and make the strength to your own taste. If you want to go the whole hog, tea glasses can be bought inexpensively from most Turkish supermarkets.

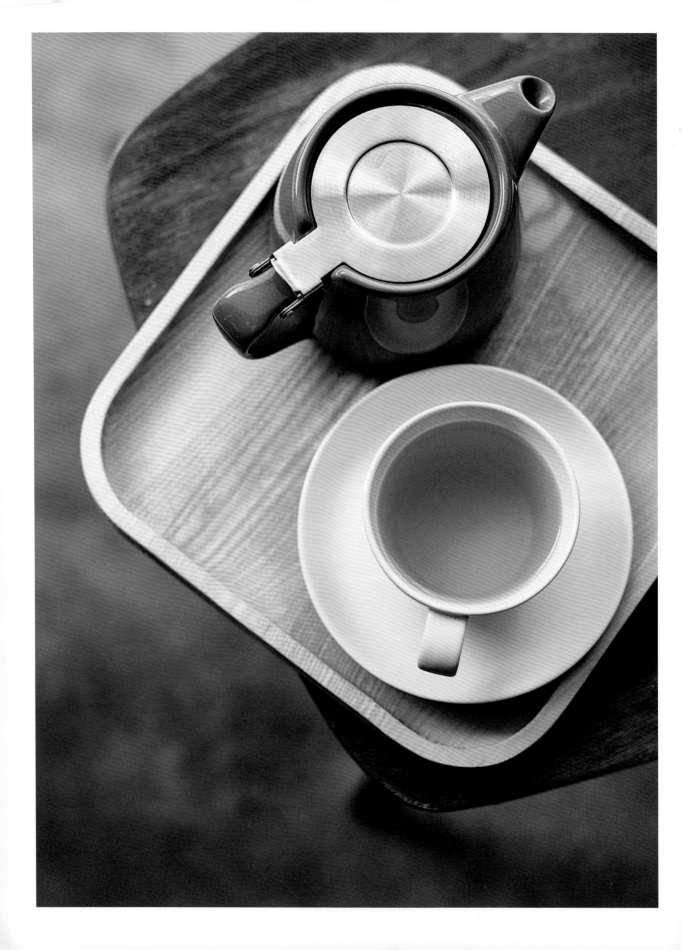

TURKISH APPLE TEA

SERVES 6

250g (9oz) apples
1.4 litres (2½ pints) boiling
    water
1 tablespoon sugar
cinnamon or cloves (optional)

As well as traditional tea, *çay*, many other kinds of tea are available in Turkey, the most popular and widely known of which is apple tea. This recipe can be enjoyed hot in traditional glasses or cups, but is equally delicious cold. To serve it cold, simply allow to cool after brewing and store in the refrigerator. Variants on this mixture are easy: you could add different spices, other fruits, replace the sugar with honey – the list goes on. The type of apples you use is up to you. I prefer green apples for a fresher taste, but red would work equally well and are perhaps a better complement to any spices, if using.

Preheat the oven to 110°C (225°F), Gas Mark ¼. Core the apples, keeping the skin on, and cut them into roughly 5mm (¼in) cubes. Spread them out on a baking sheet, making sure no cubes overlap, and bake for 1 hour, or until completely dried, shaking the tray every 15 minutes. Dried apple can be stored in an airtight container for a few months.

Pour the boiling water into a pan with the apple cubes, sugar and spices, if using. Stir until the sugar has dissolved, then simmer for about 10 minutes or slightly longer if you have added spices. To serve, strain the tea into heatproof glasses or cups.

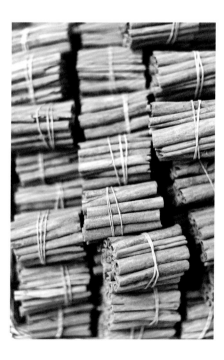

AT-HOME AYRAN

Ayran is a very popular yogurt drink in Turkey, and it's the Marmite of our soft drinks list – you either love it or hate it. People who do love it really love it, and we are frequently drunk out of stock by a single table. *Ayran* was the soft drink of choice in Turkey until the introduction of modern fizzy drinks, and although it can be drunk at any time of day, I think it's particularly well suited to brunch. If serving it to a group, I recommend putting the salt on the table for people to add to their personal taste.

SERVES 6

700ml (1¼ pints) natural
    yogurt
700ml (1¼ pints) cold water
salt
dried mint, to garnish

Beat the yogurt in a bowl by hand or with an electric mixer, gradually adding the cold water until smooth. Add enough salt to season to your taste, but keep it light so that guests can add their own. Refrigerate until required.

To serve, fill the glasses with ice and pour in the yogurt mixture. Sprinkle the dried mint on top.

TURKISH COFFEE

Turkish coffee is essentially an unfiltered, short, black coffee, often sweetened with a little sugar, but variations of it exist all across the Middle East. Like tea, coffee is very important in terms of hospitality and tradition. For example, on visiting their fiancé's family home, suitors are traditionally subjected to salt in their coffee by their potential in-laws as a test of worthiness. The practice of reading the future in coffee grounds (a popular after-dinner activity) is also Turkish in origin. Many Oklava customers can be seen turning their cup upside down on the saucer, allowing the grounds to run down and settle. No formal training is required – just interpret the shapes you see forming.

If you are planning to serve Turkish coffee regularly, it might be worth investing in some proper Turkish coffee cups – these are slightly bigger than espresso cups and available online or in Turkish supermarkets. We use Özerlat coffee in the restaurant, produced by a family business that has been roasting coffee in north Cyprus for 100 years. Iley, the great granddaughter of the company's founder, has become a great supporter of Oklava: our beautiful cups, handmade in Turkey, came via her.

To make Turkish coffee at home, you can use either a Turkish coffee pot, called a *cezve* (electric models, as well as traditional beaten copper pots, are available online) or a small milk pan. Before you start, you will need to find out if your guests would like sugar – for the uninitiated, we recommend half a teaspoon per cup – as adding sugar later disturbs the grounds and does not make for a great cup of Turkish coffee. If your guests have different sugar requirements, you will need to make their coffee in separate batches.

Add 7g (about 1 rounded teaspoon) of finely ground coffee per cup and the required amount of sugar to the pan or *cezve*, then pour in a cup of water per person, using a cup you intend to serve in, and filling it right to the brim – espresso cups work well. Put the pan on a medium heat and stir quickly and vigorously, then leave to brew until you start to see a foam form across the surface. This foam is extremely important: every good cup of Turkish coffee is covered with it. That is why we recommend making a maximum of 3 cups at a time, as it is hard to get it right otherwise.

Once the foam starts to form, remove the coffee from the heat and pour a little into each cup. Return the remaining coffee to the heat and wait until it starts to gently bubble at the edges – do not let it boil. Remove from the heat as soon as you see those bubbles and top up the cups, pouring a little at a time into each one to spread the grounds and foam evenly. Serve the coffee on a saucer, without a teaspoon in order to prevent accidental stirring. The coffee will be hotter than your average espresso, so it is best to wait a few minutes for it to cool and the grounds to fully settle.

TURKISH BLOODY MARY

SERVES 6

30ml (1fl oz) freshly squeezed lemon juice

30ml (1fl oz) Worcestershire sauce

30ml (1fl oz) olive brine

30ml (1fl oz) turnip juice (salgam)

1 teaspoon Tabasco sauce

6 teaspoons fresh grated horseradish

300ml (10fl oz) good-quality vodka

600ml (20fl oz) tomato juice

TO SERVE

1 lime

25g (1oz) sumac

6 breakfast radishes

salt and coarsely ground black pepper

nigella seeds, to sprinkle

The idea for our Turkish Bloody Mary came about when we spotted a Turkish vodka on the price list of one of our suppliers. Having not even known that Turkey was a producer of vodka, we were keen to stock the spirit and, in keeping with everything else we do at Oklava, we decided to take the classic bloody Mary and make it bloody Turkish. For the recipe below you can use any good-quality vodka; the tweaks to the recipe keep the Turkish feel.

Put the lemon juice, Worcestershire sauce, olive brine, turnip juice and Tabasco in a large jug and give them a good stir. Once combined, add the fresh horseradish and tomato juice and stir again. Try the mixture at this point to ensure the spice level is to your taste; you can add more Tabasco as required.

———

Cut the lime into wedges and rub one around the top of each serving glass. Spread the sumac out on a shallow saucer and dip the rim of each glass into it, turning to coat. If you want to keep this spicy edge looking neat, a paper napkin can be used to straighten up any wobbly bits. Make a small slit in the side of each radish, without cutting all the way though.

———

To serve, fill each glass with ice and add 50ml (2fl oz) of the vodka. Add enough of the the tomato mixture to half fill the glass, then stir; fill it to the top and stir again. Add a pinch of salt and pepper, a sprinkle of nigella seeds and balance a radish to on the rim of the glass.

POMEGRANATE & SUMAC MARTINI

This recipe is a twist on that 1990s classic, the Cosmopolitan. The pomegranate tea we use is from a company called T2 and is available online, but you can use any loose-leaf pomegranate tea for the same effect.

While the pomegranate tea is still hot, add the sugar, stir to dissolve and leave to cool overnight. At the same time, add 15g (½oz) of the sumac to the vodka and leave it overnight to infuse. About 1 hour before serving, strain the vodka and add the rum, pomegranate juice and tea syrup. Store it in the refrigerator until required.

———

To serve, fill your cocktail glasses with ice and water, leave to chill for 2 minutes, then empty them. Cut 1 lime into wedges and use it to rub around the top of the glasses. Spread out the remaining sumac in a shallow saucer, then dip the rim of each glass into it, turning to coat the whole rim. If you want to keep the sumac edge looking neat, use a paper napkin to straighten up any wobbly bits.

———

It's best to make no more than 2 cocktails at a time. To do this, fill a cocktail shaker (or any large screwtop jar) with ice. Add 250ml (9fl oz) of the prepared mixture and the juice of 1 lime. Shake well, until the shaker feels cold to the touch. Strain into the glasses, making sure the ice stays in the shaker. Repeat to make the rest of the cocktails.

SERVES 6

120ml (3¾fl oz) pomegranate tea, brewed according to the manufacturer's instructions

2–3 tablespoons sugar, to taste

40g (1½oz) sumac

150ml (5fl oz) good-quality vodka

150ml (5fl oz) spiced rum

300ml (10fl oz) pomegranate juice

1 lime, plus the freshly squeezed juice of 3 limes

MEDJOOL DATE, ESPRESSO & FENNEL MARTINI

SERVES 6

½ tablespoon fennel seeds

125g (4½oz) dried dates

175ml (6fl oz) boiling water

150ml (5fl oz) good-quality vodka

150ml (5fl oz) brandy

350ml (12fl oz) espresso or strong coffee

candied dates, to garnish (optional)

Espresso martinis have become a staple of cocktail lists across London, and we have added our own Oklava touch. At the restaurant we use a Cypriot brandy called Anglias, which is available online, but any good-quality brandy would do. If you don't have an espresso machine, we recommend brewing a strong, full-bodied coffee in a cafetière and letting it sit for 30 minutes or so, straining it before use. You can add a garnish of candied date to the rim, if you like, but this requires some advance preparation: coat sliced dried dates in sugar syrup, then leave them to harden and cool.

Toast the fennel seeds gently in a dry pan over a high heat for 60–90 seconds, or until lightly coloured. Finely chop the dried dates – whizz them in the food processor if possible – and combine them in a bowl with the boiling water and the fennel seeds. Leave overnight to infuse. It should make a thick purée, but you might need to water it down slightly to give a pourable consistency.

———

To serve, for each person fill a cocktail shaker or a large screwtop jar with ice and add 25ml (¾fl oz) vodka, 25ml (¾fl oz) brandy, 60ml (2¼fl oz) espresso and 40ml (1½fl oz) date purée. Shake hard for a few minutes to create the signature foamy top, then strain into a cocktail glass, making sure no ice falls in the drink.

CYPRIOT 75

This is our take on the classic French 75 champagne cocktail. We use Cypriot brandy, but any good-quality brandy would do; the apple tea still gives it a Turkish feel. You could use our recipe for it (see page 169) or use a shop-bought sweet apple tea. We serve this cocktail in wine glasses, but you could use champagne flutes, rocks glasses or wine glasses – whatever you prefer.

When the apple tea is cool, mix it with the brandy and refrigerate until required.

———

To serve, pour 75ml (2½fl oz) of the brandy mixture into each glass and top up with 125ml (4fl oz) sparkling wine. Hang the thyme sprig over the rim or stick it in like a straw.

SERVES 6

300ml (10fl oz) apple tea, brewed according to the packet instructions

150ml (5fl oz) brandy

700ml (1¼ pints) sparkling wine (we recommend Turkish, of course)

6 sprigs of thyme

RAKI

Rakı (pronounced 'rack-ur') is considered by many to be the national drink of Turkey, and is famous world over. Produced by distilling grape pomace and flavoured with aniseed, rakı is similar to other famous drinks from neighbouring countries, and has a somewhat fearsome reputation outside Turkey thanks to its nickname, 'lion's milk'. Although we might more commonly think of spirits as a digestif, rakı is a popular aperitif and is also often drunk throughout a meal. We serve it at the restaurant as an aperitif, with cold water and ice cubes on the side; when water is added, the liquid will turn cloudy, an effect that led to its nickname.

Rakı is often grouped with certain spirits that many of us 'enjoyed' ill-advisedly as teenagers, such as sambuca and ouzo. As a result, we find that some guests are reluctant to try it, but the addition of water brings out a softer, sweeter side to the spirit, and it is sure to be a talking point at any meal. Traditionally, rakı is drunk alongside meze or fish and is said to have been a favourite of the founder and first president of the Republic of Turkey, Mustafa Kemal Atatürk. We serve Yeni rakı, which is one of the most famous brands and widely available all over the world. It is a new style of rakı with a distinctive bitter taste, and we recommend putting a bottle of it on the dinner table, along with a jug of water and a small ice bucket, to accompany your starters and tempt your guests into trying something new.

DRESSINGS,
DIPS & BITS

MEDJOOL DATE BUTTER

The secret is finally revealed! No one has ever been able to work out what the magic flavour in our butter is, and fair enough: since my food is all about Turkish flavours, you'd never expect it to be black rice vinegar. I first made this when some friends of mine were coming over for a final meal before heading back to New Zealand. They are two big lovers of bread and butter, so I wanted to produce the most delicious butter I could make. Looking around for inspiration, I spotted some Medjool dates sitting in a black vinegar syrup, so I decided to blitz some into a block of butter. A year or so later, after serving it at one of my first pop-ups, I realized it was a huge hit: everyone kept asking for more and I ended up running out, even though I'd made twice as much as I thought I needed.

Put the dates with the sugar and vinegar in a small pan over a medium heat and cook until slightly jam like; crush the dates a little as you go. Allow the date mixture to cool completely, then combine it with the soft butter. Transfer it to a container or mould and leave to set in the refrigerator. Serve with a little flaky sea salt sprinkled on top.

MAKES ABOUT 700G (1LB 9OZ)

200g (7oz) Medjool dates, pitted

15g (½oz) caster sugar

35ml (1¼fl oz) black rice vinegar (available in Asian supermarkets)

500g (1lb 2oz) unsalted butter, softened

flaky sea salt

CHILLI BUTTER

Olive oil is widely used in Turkish cooking, but in certain parts of Turkey, butter is the leading fat in the kitchen.

Melt the butter in a pan over a medium heat and keep it there until it turns nut brown. Strain it through a fine sieve into a large heatproof container and add the chilli flakes immediately (it will puff up, hence the need for a large container). Stir in the olive oil, then set aside to cool completely before storing in the refrigerator.

MAKES ABOUT 250G (9OZ)

250g (9oz) unsalted butter

2 tablespoons Turkish chilli flakes (pul biber)

50ml (2fl oz) extra-virgin olive oil

LIME MAYONNAISE

We serve lime mayonnaise alongside our chilli-garlic chicken; the subtle zing is a real winner. If you're short on time, you could just buy a good-quality lime pickle instead of making your own.

First make the lime pickle: you will need a pressure cooker. Mix the limes with the salt in a non-reactive container and put in the refrigerator for 5 days, stirring once a day. Rinse the limes with cold water and set aside.

Put the sugar in the pressure cooker and heat, uncovered, until it forms a dark brown caramel. Remove the pan from the heat and add the mustard and coriander seeds. As they start to pop, carefully add the limes, as the mixture will spit. Cook over a medium heat for about 5 minutes, or until you see the juice coming out of the limes.

Put the lid on and gently bring the pan up to pressure. When you hear it hissing, reduce the heat to its lowest setting and cook for 15 minutes. Remove the pan from the heat and allow the pressure to drop completely before opening the lid. Add the vinegar and continue to cook, uncovered, until it is the consistency of chutney. Allow it to cool, then roughly blitz in a food processor before transferring it to a sterilized jar. Store in the refrigerator.

To make the mayonnaise, whisk the egg yolks with the mustard, vinegar and lime juice until well incorporated. (You can do this with hand-held electric beaters or by hand with a balloon whisk.) While continuing to whisk, slowly drizzle in the oil. Finish by adding the lime pickle and season with salt.

MAKES 500ML
(18FL OZ)

2 large egg yolks
½ teaspoon Dijon mustard
25ml (¾fl oz) white wine vinegar
freshly squeezed juice of ½ lime
300ml (10fl oz) sunflower oil
fine salt

FOR THE LIME PICKLE
10 limes, cut into quarters
30g (1oz) fine salt
150g (5½oz) caster sugar
20g (¾oz) black mustard seeds
20g (¾oz) coriander seeds, lightly crushed
100ml (3½fl oz) red wine vinegar

URFA CHILLI MAYONNAISE

This mayonnaise totally surprised me when we first made it, because the urfa chilli gives it an almost coffee-like flavour in the background. Serve with any meats or poultry, or even to dress a potato salad.

Put the egg yolks, vinegar, garlic and urfa chilli in a food processor and blend together well. With the motor still running, slowly drizzle in the oil until a mayonnaise is formed. Season with salt.

MAKES 1KG (2LB 4OZ)

150g (5½oz) egg yolks
80ml (2¾fl oz) moscatel vinegar
½–1 garlic clove
4 tablespoons urfa chilli flakes (isot biber)
800ml (28fl oz) sunflower oil
fine salt

BLACK OLIVE & PEPPER TAPENADE

SERVES 4–6

6 tablespoons extra-virgin olive oil

2 garlic cloves, thinly sliced

1 teaspoon thyme, leaves only

2 tablespoons sherry vinegar or red wine vinegar

4 heaped tablespoons black olive paste

2 heaped tablespoons Turkish hot pepper paste (açi biber salçasi)

fine salt

Black olive paste is available in Turkish supermarkets. It's great as part of a breakfast spread – I love it on hot toast.

Heat the oil and garlic gently in a small saucepan. When the garlic starts to turn a little brown around the edges, take the pan off the heat and add the thyme and vinegar. Combine with the two pastes, then season with salt. This will keep in the refrigerator for up to 3 weeks.

TOMATO RELISH

MAKES 300G (10½OZ)

1 banana shallot, finely diced

small bunch of chives, thinly sliced

2 sprigs of tarragon, leaves only, finely chopped

1 teaspoon urfa chilli flakes (isot biber)

200g (7oz) tomato ketchup

1 teaspoon caster sugar

2 tablespoons moscatel vinegar

80ml (2¾oz) sunflower oil

fine salt

This is essentially glorified ketchup, and it goes really well with anything meaty or fishy.

Whisk together all the ingredients and season with salt. The relish will keep for up to 3 weeks in a clean, well-sealed jar.

MUHAMMARA

My recipe is slightly different from most in that I don't use roasted peppers, but add plenty of pepper paste instead. I love Turkish pepper paste – it's so versatile. Serve *muhammara* as a dip, on toast or any way you like.

Put all the ingredients except the olive oil and salt in a food processor and blend to a coarse purée. With the motor still running, slowly drizzle in the olive oil. Season with salt.

—

The muhammara will keep up for up to a month in a clean, well-sealed jar.

MAKES 1KG

(2LB 4OZ)

250g (9oz) walnuts, toasted

50g (1¾oz) fresh breadcrumbs

75g (2¾oz) Turkish sweet pepper paste (tatli biber salçasi)

1½ garlic cloves

1 tablespoon Turkish chilli flakes (pul biber)

1 teaspoon ground cumin

freshly squeezed juice of 1 lemon

50g (1¾oz) pomegranate molasses

15g (½oz) caster sugar

375ml (12½fl oz) extra-virgin olive oil

fine salt

WHIPPED FETA

This is great as part of a meze platter or, as we serve it, on some crostini topped with a slice of candied pumpkin and sprinkled with Turkish chilli flakes (pul biber) and shredded mint. Finish the crostini with flaky sea salt and a drizzle of olive oil.

Blend the cheese and double cream to a smooth consistency in a food processor. Store in an airtight container in the refrigerator for up to 1 week.

MAKES 500G

(1LB 2OZ)

400g (14oz) Turkish white cheese or feta, crumbled

200ml (7fl oz) double cream

Opposite: *Muhammara (top left) served as a dip with flatbread, and Whipped Feta, topped with candied pumpkin, Turkish chilli flakes (pul biber) and shredded mint.*

BAHARAT

MAKES ABOUT 90G
(3¼OZ)

30g (1oz) allspice berries

30g (1oz) cloves

15g (½oz) mahlep (dried cherry seeds, available at Turkish supermarkets)

1 x 10g (¼oz) piece of nutmeg

1 x 5g (¹/₈oz) piece of mastic

Baharat is often sold as 'mixed spice' in Turkish supermarkets. This recipe is based on my grandma's, and is what she uses in her bread. I started off using it just in bread too, although I have now found other great ways to use it. It goes particularly well with fish.

This recipe features some unusual ingredients. Mahlep are dried cherry seeds, which have a bitter flavour but are great when used in the right proportion. Mastic is the resin from the mastic tree. It has a very unusual taste – almost like pine – and works very well in bread, as it gives it great elasticity. It's quite expensive, but you don't need a lot. You can leave out these ingredients if you can't find them.

——

Blend together all the spices in a spice grinder until fine. Alternatively, if you don't have a spice grinder, buy what you can find in ground form, and grind what you can't using a pestle and mortar. Stored in an airtight container, this will keep for up to 4 weeks.

SUMAC DRESSING

This is the dressing we use for our chilli-roasted cauliflower, but it would also be great as a salad dressing.

Put all the ingredients in a blender and process until smooth. Stored in the refrigerator, this dressing will keep for up to 3 weeks.

MAKES 350ML (12FL OZ)

3 garlic cloves, finely grated

freshly squeezed juice of 2 lemons

300ml (10fl oz) extra-virgin olive oil

1 tablespoon sumac

fine salt

CAPER DRESSING

This dressing has a great zing to it. Spoon it over roast lamb, chicken or even a piece of fish. My favourite pairing is with the Grilled Quails (see page 76).

Mix all the ingredients together and it's ready to go. Stored in the refrigerator, this dressing will keep for 1 week.

MAKES 150G (5½OZ)

4 tablespoons Lilliput capers, rinsed and roughly chopped

3 tablespoons caster sugar

6 tablespoons moscatel vinegar

1 banana shallot, finely diced

small bunch of mint, leaves only, chopped

small bunch of coriander, leaves and stalks, chopped

3 tablespoons extra-virgin olive oil

POMEGRANATE DRESSING

**MAKES 650ML
(23FL OZ)**

115ml (3¾fl oz) pomegranate
molasses
250ml (9fl oz) turnip juice
(salgam)
250ml (9fl oz) extra-virgin
olive oil
40ml (1½fl oz) red wine
vinegar
fine salt

We use this dressing at the restaurant for all the salads that accompany the pides and lahmacun. Our salads are a thing of beauty, if you ask me: we combine a selection of bitter and sweet leaves, herbs, onions, tomatoes, radishes, marinated olives, pickled red cabbage and anything else that's wonderful and in season. The dressing brings out all those flavours to give a zingy hit and cut through the richness of the pides. However, I would highly recommend coating any salad with this dressing, with or without pides.

Put all the ingredients in a blender and process until smooth. Taste to check the seasoning. Stored in the refrigerator, this dressing will keep for up to 4 weeks.

SHERRY VINEGAR CARAMEL

**MAKES 300ML
(10FL OZ)**

750ml (27fl oz) sherry vinegar
200g (7oz) caster sugar
400g (14fl oz) water

I love mixing acidic and sweet flavours. This caramel is a perfect balance of the two, and is great drizzled over many savoury dishes, to give them a boost of flavour. Try it with grilled fish, or a ragout of chickpeas or beans.

Put the vinegar and sugar in a pan with the water and bring to the boil. Simmer to reduce it to a light syrup.

When you think it is ready, drizzle a little onto a plate and put it in the refrigerator for 5 minutes to test it. If the syrup just holds its shape on the plate without running too much, it is ready.

MARINATED OLIVES

My mum is obsessed with green olives from Cyprus. She would often bring back as many as she could carry from her summer visits, then prepare them in batches using this recipe. I love dipping bread into all the juices.

Mix all the ingredients together in a large, sterilized screwtop jar or airtight container and leave to macerate for at least 1 day before eating. The olives will keep for up to 3 weeks.

MAKES 1KG
(2LB 4OZ)

500g (1lb 2oz) black olives (preferably Turkish), rinsed

500g (1lb 2oz) green olives (preferably Turkish), rinsed

4 tablespoons dried oregano, preferably wild

4 garlic cloves, lightly crushed

500ml (18fl oz) extra-virgin olive oil

zest (in strips) and freshly squeezed juice from 2 lemons

2 tablespoons coriander seeds, toasted and lightly crushed

PICKLED RED CABBAGE

We use this in the salad that is served with all our *pides*. I like to use this pickle recipe for any vegetables, not just red cabbage: simply pour the pickling liquid over your chosen veg while still hot and leave for a minimum of 3 days.

Put the water in a pan along with 750ml (27fl oz) of the vinegar, the sugar, spices and salt and bring to the boil. Simmer for 5 minutes. Remove from the heat and add the remaining vinegar. Strain over the red cabbage and cover with a lid. Once cool, transfer it to a sterilized jar and store in the refrigerator for 3 days before eating. The pickled cabbage will keep for up to 8 weeks.

MAKES 2KG
(4LB 8OZ)

2 litres (3½ pints) water
1 litre (1¾ pints) cider vinegar
500g (1lb 2oz) caster sugar
6 cloves
2 star anise
1 tablespoon fine salt
1 red cabbage, thinly sliced
   (preferably using a
   mandoline)

FRIED DRIED CHILLI YOGURT

MAKES 500G

(1LB 2OZ)

1 tablespoon sunflower oil

2 tablespoons extra-virgin olive oil

2 hot dried red chillies

500ml (18fl oz) Turkish or Greek yogurt

freshly squeezed juice of ½ lemon

fine salt

This is inspired by the delicious (and very hot) fried dried chillies that are served alongside fried liver in the city of Edirne.

Heat the sunflower oil in a small frying pan over a high heat. Add the chillies and cook until they change colour, turn a little darker and become crisp. Allow to cool, then roughly chop them.

———

Once cooled, place in a bowl, whisk in the remaining ingredients and season with salt.

ÇEMEN

MAKES 1KG

(2LB 4OZ)

25g (1oz) ground fenugreek

4 garlic cloves, peeled

40g (1½oz) caster sugar

75g (2¾oz) paprika

25g (1oz) hot smoked paprika

50g (2oz) sweet smoked paprika

10g (¼oz) ground cumin

50ml (1¾fl oz) extra-virgin olive oil

300ml (10fl oz) water

Çemen **is Turkish for fenugreek but the word is also used to refer to this spice paste. It is is most commonly eaten as part of** *Kayseri pastirma***, a type of cured beef that is salted, pressed and air-dried before being smeared all over with** *çemen* **and left to cure. I adore it and struggle to stop eating it once I have started. I have figured out that the thing I love most about** *pastirma* **is the flavour of the** *çemen***, so I have made my own version and now use it in all sorts of recipes.**

Put the fenugreek in bowl, pour in enough water to cover by 2.5cm (1 inch) and stir together. Leave to soak for 10 minutes, then drain off the excess water. Put the fenugreek and all the remaining ingredients in a food processor – it's best to add the garlic first, then put everything else on top – and blend to a fine purée. The paste will keep for up to 3 months, stored in an airtight container in the refrigerator.

ORANGE CREAM

We use this orange cream at the restaurant as an accompaniment to our Chocolate Delice (see page 212). When they're in season, we like to use bergamot oranges to make it.

Put the orange zest, milk and 50ml (2fl oz) of the cream in a pan and bring to the boil. Meanwhile, whisk the eggs, egg yolk, sugar and cornflour until pale and fluffy. Still whisking, pour the hot milk mixture into the egg mixture. Return it to the pan and cook, whisking continuously, over a medium heat for 4–5minutes, or until thickened and the cornflour has cooked out. Take the pan off the heat and add the butter in 3 batches, ensuring that each batch melts in before adding the next.

———

Soak the gelatine in cold water until soft, then add it to the warm custard mixture, whisking until it dissolves. Strain through a fine sieve and allow it to cool completely. Whip the remaining double cream to soft peaks. Finally, stir the orange juice into the custard mixture and fold in the whipped cream.

MAKES 800G
(1LB 12OZ)

grated zest and juice of 2 oranges (bergamot or blood oranges can be used, if available)
400ml (14fl oz) milk
175ml (6fl oz) double cream
2 large eggs, plus 1 large egg yolk
75g (2¾oz) caster sugar
60g (2¼oz) cornflour
100g (3½oz) unsalted butter, diced
2 gelatine leaves

ORANGE BLOSSOM SYRUP

This syrup is great on French toast, pancakes or any lovely Turkish dessert that calls for syrup.

Put all the ingredients, except the orange blossom water, in a pan and bring to the boil. Simmer until it reaches a syrupy consistency. Remove from the heat and add the orange blossom water. Leave the spices in to keep infusing until you use the syrup. Stored in the refrigerator, this syrup will keep for up to 3 months.

MAKES 250ML
(9FL OZ)

250g (9oz) caster sugar
2 teaspoons vanilla extract
5g (⅛oz) cloves
5g (⅛oz) star anise
140ml (4½fl oz) water
1–2 tablespoons orange blossom water

PRESERVED LEMONS

MAKES 1.5KG
(3LB 5OZ)

10 lemons, quartered
50g (1¾oz) fine salt
25g (1oz) flaky sea salt
2 bay leaves
4 sprigs of thyme

Preserved lemons are readily available these days, but it's so easy to make your own. I highly recommend trying this recipe and stashing them away to jazz up your meals.

Mix all the ingredients together, slightly squishing the lemons as you go. Put them in a sterilized jar or lidded container, seal tightly and put them in the refrigerator. Leave to macerate for 4 weeks, turning the container upside down every day. The lemons will keep for up to 3 months.

SEMOLINA CUSTARD & FILO BÖREK

You can serve these pastries as they are (they're best slightly warm), or with some ice cream and a few pistachios for extra indulgence. The recipe for _sütlü börek_ I've given here is a slight variation of one of my mum's, to which I've added vanilla and orange blossom because I think it tastes nicer. Mum isn't convinced, and thinks that the traditional way is the best, so I invite you to try it both ways and judge for yourself.

First make the syrup: put the water in a pan with the sugar and bring to the boil. Simmer until it takes on a syrupy consistency and is slightly sticky. Add the lemon juice and the orange blossom water, if using. Leave to cool completely.

———

To make the filling, mix the semolina and cornflour with about 200ml (7fl oz) of the milk to make a smooth paste. Put the remaining milk in a pan with the sugar and heat to just below boiling point. Whisk the semolina mixture into the hot milk and reduce the heat to medium. Add the vanilla and keep whisking until you have a very thick custard. Immediately pour it into a shallow tray measuring about 40 x 30cm (16 x 12in). Allow the mixture to cool, then cut it, still in the tray, into 18–20 equal rectangular pieces.

———

Preheat the oven to 220°C (425°F), Gas Mark 7 and line 2 large baking sheets with baking parchment. Take 1 sheet of filo pastry and fold it in half to form a small rectangle. Place it on the work surface portrait way up. Brush it all over with butter. Now place a rectangle of the custard in the middle of the edge closest to you and fold it over once, working away from you, to enclose it in the pastry. Fold in each side of the pastry on the left and right. Brush the sides with butter and continue folding over until you reach the end of the pastry, sealing it with a little butter. It is important to fold quite tightly around the custard and ensure there are no cracks for it to escape. If any cracks do form, wrap the whole thing in another sheet of filo.

———

Place the börek on a prepared baking sheet and repeat the folding process with the rest of the filo and custard. Leave a 2cm (¾in) gap between each pastry. Brush the tops with butter and bake until golden brown all over, about 20 minutes. When you take them out of the oven, submerge them one at a time in the cold syrup and transfer to a serving dish. Sprinkle over the pistachios, if using. Allow to cool before serving.

MAKES 18–20

20 sheets of filo pastry

200g (7oz) unsalted butter, melted

100g (3½oz) pistachios, toasted and crushed (optional)

FOR THE FILLING

250g (9oz) semolina

4 heaped tablespoons cornflour

1.2 litres (2 pints) milk

3 heaped tablespoons caster sugar

1 teaspoon vanilla extract

FOR THE SYRUP

500ml (18fl oz) water

500g (1lb 2oz) caster sugar

freshly squeezed juice of ½ lemon

2 teaspoons orange blossom water (optional)

SPICED RICE PUDDING BRÛLÉE WITH PISTACHIOS, CARAMELIZED PINEAPPLE, RUM JELLY, LYCHEES & CANDIED LIME ZEST

SERVES 8–10

demerara sugar, for sprinkling

100g (3½oz) pistachios, toasted and crushed

FOR THE RICE PUDDING

1.4 litres (2½pints) milk

100g (3½oz) caster sugar

15cm (6in) cinnamon sticks

1 rounded tablespoon star anise

1 rounded tablespoon cloves

1 teaspoon vanilla extract

150g (5½oz) arborio rice

200ml (7fl oz) double cream

FOR THE RUM JELLY

25g (1oz) dark brown sugar

125ml (4fl oz) water

2 gelatine leaves

30ml (1fl oz) good-quality rum

FOR THE LYCHEES

grated zest and freshly squeezed juice of 1 lime

10g (¼oz) fresh ginger, finely grated

175g (6oz) drained tinned lychees, halved

FOR THE CANDIED LIME ZEST

2 limes

75g (2¾oz) caster sugar

50ml (2fl oz) water

FOR THE CARAMELIZED PINEAPPLE

50g (1¾oz) caster sugar

½ fresh pineapple, peeled, cored and diced into 2cm (¾in) pieces

15g (½oz) unsalted butter

35g (1¼oz) tamarind paste

This dish is inspired by *sütlaç*, a traditional creamy spiced rice pudding, and it has converted many a rice-pudding doubter. There are a lot of garnishes, but the rice pudding is tasty just on its own, so make as few or as many of the extras as you like. If you would like to make your own tamarind paste, buy fresh tamarind (with seeds), simmer them in water until soft, then pass through a sieve.

First make the rice pudding: put the milk, sugar, spices and vanilla in a pan and bring gently to a simmer. Remove from the heat and cover the pan with clingfilm. Leave to infuse for 30 minutes. Strain the milk into a new pan and add the rice. Cook, stirring occasionally, over a low heat for about 30 minutes, or until the rice is soft. Leave the rice to cool (it will still look quite liquid but will firm up), then chill completely.

Whip the cream to soft peaks and fold it through the cooled rice pudding. Divide between 8–10 ramekins or bowls and return to the refrigerator until needed.

To make the rum jelly, put the sugar and water in a pan, bring to the boil and simmer for 2 minutes. Put the gelatine into cold water to soften. Remove the pan from the heat and add the rum and gelatine, stirring to dissolve. Strain into a container, leave to cool, then store in the refrigerator.

To make the lychees, mix the ingredients in a bowl, then set aside.

To make the candied lime zest, peel the limes, scrape off the pith and slice the zest into very fine strips. Put the sugar and water in a pan and bring to the boil. Add the strips of lime zest, reduce the heat to a very gentle simmer and cook until a thick syrup forms. Drain off the syrup and leave the lime zest to cool on a rack or a tray lined with baking parchment.

To make the caramelized pineapple, put the sugar in a large heavy-based pan or non-stick frying pan and add a dash of water to make a paste. Cook over a medium heat without stirring until a dark caramel forms, then immediately and carefully add the pineapple. The caramel will clump together a little, so keep cooking until it all turns liquid again. Add the butter and keep cooking until most of the liquid has evaporated. Add the tamarind paste, transfer to a container and leave to cool.

To assemble, sprinkle a thin layer of demerara sugar evenly over each rice pudding. Use a blowtorch or very hot grill to caramelize the sugar golden-brown. Allow the caramelized sugar to cool, then sprinkle over the pistachios, followed by some pineapple and lychees. Now place 4–5 small spoonfuls of rum jelly on each pudding. Finish with a few strands of candied lime zest.

TRILECE CAKE

I first tried *trilece* cake in Istanbul when it was brought to us as a complimentary dessert by a waiter who was very much taken with Laura. I thought it was delicious, and the waiter told me it was a traditional Balkan dessert. I later found out that this cake is in fashion in Istanbul, with restaurants across the city trying to out-do each other with their versions. The cake is almost biscuit-like once baked, so quite a dry texture, but this allows it to soak up all the flavour from the milk to produce a delicious moist sponge. I like to serve this cake with some Medjool dates, which I coat in a little of the caramel topping and finish with a dollop of *kaymak* (clotted cream).

Preheat the oven to 200°C (400°F), Gas Mark 6 and grease a 30 x 25 x 5cm (12 x 10 x 2in) baking tray, or 12 individual baking rings, 8cm (3¼in) diameter.

———

Whisk the egg whites to soft peaks in a large bowl. Add the sugar in 3 batches, whisking constantly to ensure that each batch is fully incorporated before adding the next. Whisk in the egg yolks one at a time, followed by the vanilla extract.

———

Fold in the flour and baking powder until fully incorporated. I use a whisk to do this, but folding rather than whisking. Carefully pour the batter into the prepared tray or rings and bake until golden brown and springy. Individual cakes will take about 12 minutes and a whole tray will take about 30 minutes.

———

While the cake bakes, mix together the ingredients for the soaking liquid. When the cake comes out of the oven, pour the cold mixture over the hot sponge and allow it to cool completely and absorb the liquid for about 4 hours. Once cool, cut the cake into 12 equal pieces.

———

To make the caramel, put the glucose and sugar in a heavy-based pan or non-stick frying pan and cook over a medium heat until it becomes a dark caramel. Taking great care, as it will spit, slowly pour in the water. The caramel will seize up, but keep cooking until it all turns to liquid again. Continue heating the caramel until it becomes a fairly thick syrup. To test it, pour a little onto a saucer and place in the fridge for 5 minutes – the caramel should still be a little runny once cool. If it isn't, it has gone too far, so add a little more water and bring it back up the boil. Allow the caramel to cool completely before pouring it over the cake, keeping back a little to garnish each serving. To serve, put a piece of cake on each plate and drizzle a little extra caramel around it. Add some Medjool dates dipped in caramel, then top with a dollop of cream.

SERVES 12

sunflower oil, for greasing
4 large eggs, separated
200g (7oz) caster sugar
2 teaspoons vanilla extract
270g (9¾oz) plain flour, sifted
1½ teaspoons baking powder, sifted

FOR THE SOAKING LIQUID

500ml (18fl oz) cow's, goat's or sheep's milk
250ml (9fl oz) double cream
250ml (9fl oz) condensed milk

FOR THE CARAMEL

300g (10½oz) glucose
150g (5½oz) caster sugar
240ml (8½fl oz) water

TO SERVE

Medjool dates
kaymak (clotted cream)

DARK CHOCOLATE & PRALINE KATMER WITH PISTACHIOS

SERVES 1–2

1 sheet of filo pastry, about 37 x 30cm (14½ x 12in)

30g (1oz) unsalted butter, melted

5 teaspoons praline paste or Nutella

15g (½oz) good-quality dark chocolate (70% cocoa solids), roughly chopped

40g (1½oz) shelled pistachios, toasted and chopped

Praline is one of my guilty pleasures, particularly in the form of a certain sea shell chocolate. *Katmer* **is a speciality dish from Gaziantep in south-eastern Anatolia, traditionally filled with** *kaymak*, **which is a bit like clotted cream, and pistachios, and often served as a breakfast dish alongside a cup of Turkish tea. Traditionally the pastry is hand-made by expert bakers, who stretch it out thinner than a bedsheet before folding it into a multi-layered square with the filling in the centre. Using ready-made filo pastry makes this recipe much more feasible for the non-expert, and the chocolate and praline filling makes it a perfect indulgent weekend brunch dish. This recipe makes just one** *katmer*, **but it is easily scaled up to make as many as you desire.**

Brush the filo sheet with a little of the melted butter. Place the praline in 5 dots in a square formation in the centre of the sheet. Sprinkle over the chocolate and half the pistachios.

———

Starting at the top left, fold the corner into the centre, then fold the bottom right corner in to meet it. Fold in the two remaining corners, overlapping them in the middle to end up with a square.

———

Place a large frying pan over a medium-high heat and add the remaining melted butter. Place the katmer in the pan, seam-side down. Cook for 1–2 minutes on each side, or until golden and crisp. Serve with the rest of the pistachios sprinkled over the top.

CHOCOLATE, PRUNE
& CARDAMOM DELICE

This rich layered dessert, gently spiced with cardamom, will appeal to chocoholics and fans of fruity desserts alike.

First make the poached prunes: put the water in a pan with the sugar, mastic, vanilla, orange zest, wine and tea leaves and bring to the boil. Simmer until it reaches a light syrup consistency. Strain into a container, add the prunes and leave to steep for at least 1 hour. Strain off the liquid into a pan and simmer to reduce to a thick syrup. Process half the prunes to a coarse purée using a stick blender, and set aside. Put the rest of the prunes into a container, pour over the thick syrup and set aside.

———

Place a stainless steel cake frame, about 30 x 20cm (12 x 8in), on a tray lined with baking parchment.

———

To make the praline, break the milk chocolate and 75g (2¾oz) of the dark chocolate into pieces and put it in a heatproof bowl with the praline. Set it over a pan of barely simmering water. Once the chocolate has melted, remove from the heat and stir in the feuilletine. Pour half the mixture into your frame, spread it out in an even layer, then refrigerate to set. Melt the remaining mixture with the remaining dark chocolate, then spread it in a thin layer on a baking tray lined with baking parchment. Put it in the refrigerator to cool.

———

To make the delice, put the milk, cream and cardamom in a pan and bring to the boil. Remove from the heat, cover with clingfilm and leave to infuse for 1 hour.

———

Once the praline mixture in the frame has set, spread the prune purée over it and return it to the refrigerator.

———

Break the delice chocolate into pieces and melt as before. Strain the cardamom-infused milk mixture and bring it back to the boil. Whisk the egg yolks in a bowl until pale, then slowly pour the hot milk mixture over them, whisking continuously. Return to the pan and set over a low heat, whisking until it has thickened to a custard consistency. Pour it over the melted chocolate, whisking continuously. Pour the mixture into the frame on top of the prune purée. Return it to the refrigerator to set.

———

Now make the chocolate glaze: soak the gelatine leaves in cold water until softened. Meanwhile, put the water, cream, sugar and cocoa in a pan and whisk together. Bring to the boil, whisking all the time, until slightly sticky. Remove the pan from the heat, add the gelatine and whisk until dissolved. Strain into a bowl and allow to cool to room temperature.

———

Evenly spread the glaze over the delice. Return to the refrigerator to set. Using a blowtorch, heat the frame just enough to release it and lift it off. Using a hot knife, cut the delice into 16–24 pieces. Serve the delice with the whole prunes, shards of praline, a dollop of orange cream and a drizzle of leftover glaze, if you have some.

SERVES 16–24

140ml (4½fl oz) milk

325ml (11fl oz) double cream

5g (⅛oz) cardamom pods, toasted and crushed

340g (11¾oz) good-quality dark chocolate

120g (4¼oz) egg yolks

1 quantity Orange Cream (see page 200), to serve

FOR THE POACHED PRUNES

190ml (6½fl oz) water

75g (2¾oz) caster sugar

1g gum mastic

10g (¼oz) vanilla extract

grated zest of 1 orange, bergamot variety if possible

125ml (4fl oz) white wine

5g (⅛oz) Earl Grey tea leaves

250g (9oz) prunes

FOR THE PRALINE

75g (2¾oz) good-quality milk chocolate

125g (4½oz) good-quality dark chocolate

25g (1oz) praline paste or Nutella

100g (3½oz) feuilletine or crushed cornflakes

FOR THE CHOCOLATE GLAZE

10g (¼oz) gelatine leaves

100ml (3½fl oz) water

130ml (4½fl oz) double cream

210g (7½oz) caster sugar

90g (3¼oz) cocoa powder

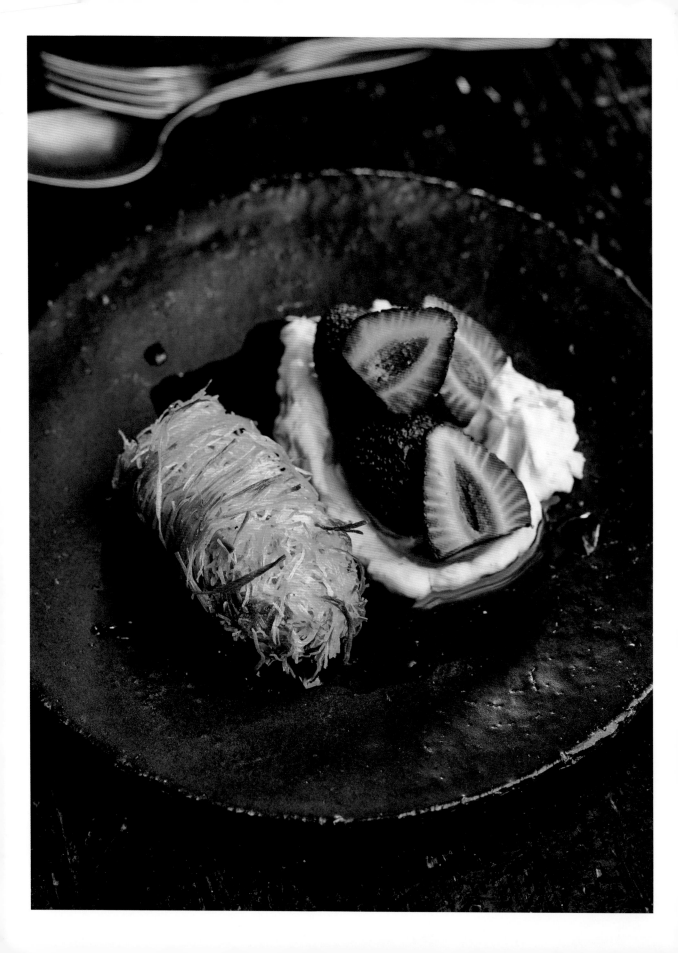

RICOTTA & VANILLA KADAYIF WITH BERGAMOT CREAM & STRAWBERRIES

SERVES 8

400g (14oz) kadayif pastry (available in Turkish supermarkets)

150g (5½oz) unsalted butter, melted

160g (5¾oz) ricotta

1 teaspoon vanilla extract

1 quantity Orange Blossom Syrup (see page 200)

16 strawberries, hulled and halved

FOR THE BERGAMOT CREAM

160g (5¾oz) mascarpone

grated zest of ½ orange

½ teaspoon vanilla extract

1 heaped tablespoon candied bergamot (available online), finely chopped, or bergamot jam

Kadayif is best described as shredded filo pastry, and it is used in many ways to create syrup-based desserts. You're aiming for a pastry that is soaked in syrup but retains some crunch; it shouldn't be soggy. The bergamot cream adds sharpness and the strawberries a freshness to balance out the indulgence of the syrupy ricotta pastry.

Preheat the oven to 220°C (425°F), Gas Mark 7.

Put the pastry into a bowl, pour in the melted butter and mix very well. Divide the pastry into 8 equal piles, arranging each pile into a long rectangle.

Mix the ricotta with the vanilla, divide into 8 equal portions and place one at the end of each pastry rectangle. Roll up tightly to form 8 cylinders. Place on a baking tray, seam-side down. Bake for 18–20 minutes, or until golden brown and crisp.

Meanwhile, combine all the ingredients for the bergamot cream.

Remove the pastries from the oven and pour the cold orange blossom syrup all over them, reserving a little syrup to serve. Allow to cool slightly before serving with a spoonful of bergamot cream, a pile of strawberries and an extra drizzle of orange blossom syrup.

SEMOLINA CAKE

Simit tatlisi is a classic cake in our household. Mum makes it at the end of the Bayram dinners that mark Turkish festivals and national holidays. At Bayram, all the family comes together for a big Turkish roast dinner with all the trimmings. This recipe is slightly lighter and not quite as sweet as a traditional version, which is just as well at the end of a big meal.

First make the syrup. Bring the water and sugar to the boil in a pan. Reduce the heat and simmer until it reaches a syrupy consistency, then add the lemon juice and rose or orange blossom water, if using. Set aside to cool.

——

Preheat the oven to 220°C (425°F), Gas Mark 7 and lightly oil a baking dish measuring about 26 x 36cm (10 x 14in).

——

To make the cake, put the eggs, vanilla, sugar and lemon zest in a bowl and whisk until just combined. Add the measured oil and milk. Mix the semolina and baking powder together in a large bowl. Gradually, whisking all the time, add the wet mixture to the semolina to form a smooth batter. Pour it into the prepared dish and scatter the almonds over the surface. Bake for about 30 minutes, or until golden brown and an inserted skewer comes out cleanly.

——

Leave the cake to rest for 2 minutes before pouring over the syrup in 4 batches, allowing each batch to be absorbed before adding the next. Once all the syrup has been absorbed, cut the cake into portions.

SERVES 16–20

190ml (6½fl oz) sunflower oil, plus extra for greasing

4 large eggs

1 teaspoon vanilla extract

250g (9oz) caster sugar

grated zest of 1 lemon

250ml (9fl oz) milk

500g (1lb 2oz) coarse semolina

1 tablespoon baking powder

200g (7oz) skinned whole almonds, crushed

FOR THE SYRUP

1.5 litres (2½ pints) water

500g (1lb 2oz) caster sugar

freshly squeezed juice of ¼ lemon

1–2 tablespoons rose water or orange blossom water (optional)

BLOOD ORANGE GANACHE, POACHED PEAR & ROSEMARY FILO SHARDS

SERVES 8

500ml (18fl oz) blood orange juice

270g (9½oz) good-quality white chocolate

200ml (7fl oz) double cream

½ teaspoon vanilla extract

FOR THE POACHED PEAR

1 litre (1¾ pints) water

250ml (9fl oz) white wine

375g (13oz) caster sugar

250g (9oz) honey

1 strip of lemon zest

1 sprig of thyme

4 pears (I like to use Williams)

freshly squeezed juice of ½ lemon

FOR THE DECORATION

4 sheets of filo pastry

3 heaped tablespoons unsalted butter

icing sugar, for dusting

1 tablespoon rosemary, finely chopped

2 blood oranges, segmented

This blood orange ganache is a real crowd pleaser. It's rich and works well alongside the juicy poached pear and the filo shards that add texture to the dish. At the beginning of the year, when blood oranges are in season, I always include this on the menu.

Bring the orange juice to the boil in a pan and simmer to reduce it to 150ml (5fl oz). Meanwhile, put the white chocolate, double cream and vanilla in a heatproof bowl set over a pan of barely simmering water, making sure the bowl doesn't touch the water. Leave it to melt, then remove from heat and let it cool slightly. Once the white chocolate mixture and reduced orange juice are about the same temperature, whisk them together. Transfer to a container and place in the refrigerator to set.

———

To poach the pears, put the water in a pan with the wine, sugar, honey, lemon zest and thyme and bring to the boil. Reduce the heat and simmer until it reaches a light syrup consistency. Meanwhile, peel the pears, cut them in half and remove the core with a spoon. Rub them with the lemon juice to prevent discoloration. Once all the pears are prepared, add them carefully to the poaching liquid and cover with a piece of baking parchment sitting directly on top of the liquid.

Reduce the heat to its lowest setting and poach for about 15 minutes, or until the pears are just soft (use a knife to test them). Remove the fruit and simmer the liquid to reduce it to a thicker syrup consistency. Set aside to cool, then pour it over the pears.

———

Preheat the oven to 220°C (425°F), Gas Mark 7. To make filo shards, take 1 sheet of filo and brush it with melted butter. Dust it with icing sugar, sprinkle over some rosemary, then place another sheet of filo over the top. Repeat the process twice more, brushing and sprinkling between each one, but brush the very top with butter only. Place the filo 'sandwich' between 2 sheets of baking parchment, then slide it onto a flat baking tray and put another (preferably identical) baking tray on top. Bake for 6 minutes, then check to see if the filo is golden brown and crisp. You will probably need to cook it for another 5 minutes, but keep checking it. Remove the top baking sheet and set the filo aside to cool.

———

To serve, put half a poached pear on each plate (if you have a blowtorch, you could lightly glaze the cut side). Put a spoonful of ganache next to the pear, break off a shard of filo and poke it into the ganache. Decorate each plate with fresh orange segments and serve.

MUHALLEBI WITH STRAWBERRY JELLY

Muhallebi is a milk pudding thickened with cornflour. It was my dad's favourite dessert, so there was often a bowl of this sitting in the refrigerator when I was growing up. Traditionally, it is served with rosewater syrup or a sprinkling of ground cinnamon. I think the addition of strawberry jelly, which is inspired by my chef college mentor Vince Cottam, is very good. Vince coached me through several culinary competitions, and a berry-based soup was sometimes included in our desserts. I've adjusted the recipe here to make the berry soup into a jelly.

In a small bowl, mix the cornflour with 200ml (7fl oz) of the milk. Put the rest of the milk in a pan and bring gently to the boil. Reduce the heat and whisk in the cornflour mixture and the sugar. Continue whisking until it turns into a thick custard, then pour it straight into your serving glasses or dishes and leave to cool. Once cool, put it in the refrigerator to set.

———

To make the jelly, mix the berries with the icing sugar and vanilla in a heatproof bowl and cover it tightly with clingfilm. Set the bowl over a pan of simmering water and leave for 30 minutes: the juices will be released from the fruits. Transfer to a sieve set over a jug and leave until all the juices have run out. You can push very gently on the fruits to help the process along, but don't push too hard, or the juice will become cloudy.

———

The amount of liquid released from your fruit will determine how much gelatine you need. For 100ml (3½fl oz) liquid you need 1 gelatine leaf. Soak the correct amount of gelatine in cold water until softened. Heat half the berry liquid in a pan to just below boiling point, then remove from the heat, squeeze out the gelatine and add it to the hot liquid. Once the gelatine has dissolved, whisk in the rest of the berry liquid and strain the mixture through a sieve. Once it is completely cold, divide it between the muhallebi dishes and return them to the refrigerator to set. Serve with a selection of fresh berries on top.

SERVES 4–6

3 heaped tablespoons cornflour

570ml (1 pint) milk

1 teaspoon vanilla extract

3 heaped tablespoons caster sugar

200g (7oz) mixed berries, washed and hulled, to decorate

FOR THE STRAWBERRY JELLY

150g (5½oz) raspberries, hulled

300g (10½oz) strawberries, hulled

150g (5½oz) redcurrants (or use more of the other berries)

30g (1oz) icing sugar

½ vanilla pod, halved lengthways and seeds scraped out

2–3 gelatine leaves

SYRUP SPONGE STUFFED WITH RICOTTA & WALNUTS

SERVES 10–12

1 packet ekmek kadayif
  (a kind of dry sponge
  cake, available at Turkish
  supermarkets), about 25cm
  (10 inches) in diameter,
  sliced in half horizontally

500g (1lb 2oz) ricotta

300g (10½oz) walnuts, toasted
  and crushed

50ml (2fl oz) rose water or
  orange blossom water
  (optional)

FOR THE SYRUP

1.5 litres (2½pints) water

1kg (2lb 4oz) caster sugar

2 cardamom pods, toasted
  and lightly crushed

If you are a fan of syrup-based desserts, you will love this one, called *Ekmek Kadayif* in Turkish. I especially like the way the ricotta gives it a savoury touch to balance out the sweetness. The cardamom is my addition, so not traditional; you could also try it with other spices, such as cloves, star anise and cinnamon. You can find the dried bread-like sponge used in this recipe at Turkish supermarkets or bakeries – if they don't have it and you ask nicely, they will usually make it for you. Serve with ice cream or clotted cream.

Start by making the syrup. Put the water, sugar and cardamom in a pan and bring to the boil. Reduce the heat and simmer to a light syrup consistency. Strain into a fresh pan once ready, and keep hot.

———

Meanwhile, place each sponge half, cut side up, on 2 separate trays (the bottom half should go into a large baking tray that can sit over direct heat). Spoon the rose water, if using, over each half. Spread the ricotta over the bottom layer of the sponge, and sprinkle with the walnuts. Top with the other sponge.

———

Place the tray directly over a medium heat and ladle the hot syrup over the cake bit by bit until all used up. Once the syrup has sunk to the bottom of the tray, use a tablespoon to keep basting it over until it is all absorbed. Leave to cool completely before cutting and serving.

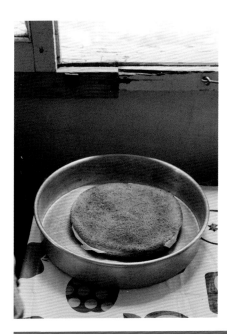

POACHED & BARBECUED QUINCE

I first discovered that this was a great way to cook fruit when I tried it with peaches, so all types of stone fruit can be prepared like this too. Quince is very popular in Turkey: it is used in jams, compotes or simply poached in syrup. My mum even likes it raw! This dish makes a lovely accompaniment to a piece of cake or tart, and is great served with ice cream and chopped pistachios, with some extra syrup poured over the top. But it also works well as a dessert on its own, especially after a barbecue.

SERVES 8

1 litre (1¾ pints) water

1kg (2lb 4oz) caster sugar

½ cinnamon stick

2 cloves

1 star anise

½ vanilla pod, halved
lengthways and seeds
scraped out

4 quinces

juice of 1 lemon

1 tablespoon orange blossom
water (optional)

Put the water in a pan with the sugar, cinnamon, cloves, star anise, vanilla seeds and pod and bring to the boil. Simmer to reduce to a light syrup consistency.

———

Meanwhile, peel the quinces, cut them into quarters, remove the core and rub the pieces with lemon juice. If your syrup is not ready to start poaching them immediately, put the quince in water with a squeeze of lemon juice.

———

Put the quince pieces in the syrup and simmer gently with a circle of baking parchment sitting directly on top of the liquid to hold the fruit down. Simmer for 8 minutes, then check to see if they are tender. You should be able to insert a knife or skewer comfortably. Don't overcook them, as they will turn to mush. Remove from the heat and leave to cool in the syrup. Add the orange blossom water, if using.

———

Heat a barbecue until ready to cook and the coals are grey, or heat a ridged griddle pan until very hot. Drain the quince pieces and place on the hot barbecue or griddle pan. Cook for 2–3 minutes, or until charred, then turn and cook the other side. Dress the quince pieces in a little syrup before serving.

CANDIED BERGAMOT & SEVILLE ORANGES

MAKES 40 PIECES

10 bergamot or Seville
   oranges
350ml (12fl oz) water
750g (1lb 10oz) caster sugar
juice of ½ lemon

Preserving fruits and even some vegetables in syrup is very common in Turkish cookery. Cyprus is especially well known for producing the best preserves: I think this is because the produce is so incredible in the first place. Some of my favourites are whole green walnuts, bergamot and Seville oranges (known in Turkish as *turunc*). Try using them in desserts to flavour creams, or even with some thick yogurt for breakfast. Traditionally, they are served on a small fork sitting inside a glass of cold water, to be eaten after a strong Turkish coffee.

Finely grate a thin layer of the zest off each fruit. Cut a small slice off the top and bottom, then slide the blade of a small knife between the pith and the flesh at the top and bottom of the fruit. Now score each orange 4 times from top to bottom, spacing the cuts evenly. Remove the 4 pieces of peel. Using a small knife, carefully remove most of the pith from inside each piece of peel.

———

To achieve a nice shape, roll up each piece of peel and pass a needle and strong cotton or string through it. Roll up the next piece and thread it onto the cotton next to the first one, pushing the pieces close together. Repeat with the rest of the peel. Alternatively, you can just leave the pieces as they are. Once they are all threaded, tie up the ends tightly.

———

Place the peel pieces in a large bowl or pan of cold water and put a plate on top to hold them down. Change the water 2–3 times during the day and repeat this process for 4–5 days. (This is to remove the bitterness.)

———

Fill a large pan with fresh water, add the peel pieces and bring to the boil. Drain and refill the pan, then bring to the boil again. Repeat this process 3 more times, then drain and leave to cool. Once they are cool enough to handle, take the peel pieces off the string.

———

Put the measured water in the pan, add the sugar and bring it to the boil, then turn it down to a simmer and add the peel pieces. Cook for 30–40 minutes, or until the liquid takes on a loose, syrup-like consistency. Add the lemon juice. Remove from the heat, then transfer the peel and syrup to sterilized jars.

TAHINI SPIRAL & SPICED HOT CHOCOLATE

This is a take on the Spanish churros and hot chocolate. The crisp, flaky pastry goes perfectly with the gently spiced chocolate. You could try using peanut butter too. For me, a trip to a Turkish bakery normally involves picking up one of these spirals. For the hot chocolate, you could play around with the spices and use cumin, vanilla, chilli or baharat (see page 193).

In a large bowl, mix together the flour, yeast, sugar and salt. Add the milk, butter, oil and egg, bring it together with your hands, then knead to make a smooth dough. Cover the bowl with clingfilm and set aside in a warm place until doubled in size (this will take about 1 hour).

———

Meanwhile, mix the tahini and sugar together. Once the dough has proved, knead it gently and divide it into 4 equal pieces. Roll each piece into a ball and cover with a damp cloth. Preheat the oven to 200°C (400°F), Gas Mark 6 and line a baking sheet with baking parchment.

———

Take one ball of dough and roll it out on a lightly floured surface into a circle about 3mm (¹/₈in) thick. Spread a quarter of the tahini mixture across the dough, leaving a 2cm (¾in) gap around the edge. Sprinkle over a quarter of the walnuts, if using. Roll the dough up tightly to make a sausage shape. Take the ends of the dough and twist in opposite directions to make a corkscrew shape, then roll the whole thing into a spiral, tucking the end in underneath. Place it on the prepared baking sheet, pushing it down evenly to flatten it a little. Repeat with the rest of the dough. You might need to use 2 baking sheets to make sure you can leave a 3cm (1¼in) gap between each spiral. Let them rest for 15 minutes.

———

Brush the tops of the spirals with the eggwash. Scatter over the extra walnuts, if using. Bake for 25–30 minutes, or until golden and crisp.

———

To make the spiced hot chocolate, put the milk and spices in a saucepan over a medium heat. Gently bring to a simmer, stirring occasionally. Turn the heat off and leave to infuse for 20 minutes. Add the chocolate and return to a low heat until melted. Add as much sugar and orange blossom water as you wish. Strain out all the spices, pour the hot chocolate into cups and grate over the nutmeg. Serve with the tahini spirals.

SERVES 4–8 (MAKES 4 LARGE SPIRALS)

1kg (2lb 4oz) plain flour, plus extra for dusting

1 x 7g sachet fast-action dried yeast

1 tablespoon caster sugar

½ teaspoon fine salt

250ml (9fl oz) milk

50g (1¾oz) unsalted butter, softened

50ml (2fl oz) sunflower oil

1 large egg

eggwash made from 1 large egg yolk beaten with 1 tablespoon milk

FOR THE FILLING

250g (9oz) tahini

250g (9oz) caster sugar

150g (5½oz) walnuts, toasted and crushed, plus extra for the tops (optional)

FOR THE SPICED HOT CHOCOLATE

1.5 litres (2½ pints) milk

1 cinnamon stick, toasted

1 tablespoon fennel seeds, toasted

1 tablespoon coriander seeds, toasted

225g (8oz) dark chocolate (70% cocoa solids), chopped

caster sugar, to taste

orange blossom water, to taste (optional)

freshly grated nutmeg, to taste

INDEX

ACKNOWLEDGEMENTS

Selin

The hospitality industry is a notoriously difficult one to work in, but it is also full of people with an enormous amount of passion and kindness. On the road to opening Oklava, a huge number of people helped us in various ways, generous with their time and expertise. It is incredibly humbling to think that so many people helped because they wanted us to succeed – thank you to all of you.

I have to specifically name some of them here though, for all of their help. So first of all I would like to thank all past and present team members at Oklava: you guys have been amazing and all worked so hard to create our beautiful little restaurant, and make mine and Laura's dream a reality.

Lucy, for always sticking by me. You were there with me from Kopapa to the pop-ups and from day one at Oklava. Your hard work and dedication make you an incredible chef and I am so proud of you.

Nick, my super sous chef, I cannot thank you enough: this book would not have materialized if not for all your hard work and many, many hours spent in the kitchen covering me. Thank you for never getting annoyed by the fact that I would sit at the bar writing this book and boss you about at the same time! I am truly honoured to have you work by my side and I couldn't do this without you.

Laura, you are an amazing business partner and I couldn't have imagined anyone better to work alongside me.

Vince Cottam, my college mentor, you kickstarted so many opportunities for me and have always believed in me.

Peter Gordon and Michael McGrath, working at The Providores was a magical time in my life, and I feel so fortunate to have worked in your restaurant. Peter, cooking in your kitchen, where I was encouraged to experiment and cook freely, has shaped me into the chef I am today. You are my hero.

Hannah Norris, you have believed in me from day one. Thank you for championing me and my cooking.

Zoe Ross for being a great support.

Chris Terry, our photographer, his assistant Danny and Cynthia Inions our prop stylist, for coming out to Cyprus to shoot all the gorgeous photos and help shape the Oklava book.
Mum, for supporting my career, inspiring so many of the recipes and coming out to Cyprus for the photo shoot to help me cook all the recipes. My sisters Sinem and Sibel, for convincing my parents it was OK for me to be a chef, and to my nieces and nephew Kayla, Joshan and Ella for being so incredibly excited about everything I do.

All of my friends, but especially Tamara, Asya, Gabby, Harshini, Ruyan, Sophie and Danielle, for your encouragement and putting up with the fact you don't see me very much as I'm always working.

Everyone at Octopus, especially Stephanie Jackson for trusting that I could write this book; I'm not quite sure why she was so convinced I could do this but her gentle powers of persuasion certainly worked. Yasia Williams for totally understanding the Oklava vision and ethos and translating it into the book and Alex Stetter for being an incredibly patient editor.

Finally, most of all I would like to thank Rebecca. You have been through this whole journey with me, supported me through highs and lows and always kept me believing that Oklava would be a reality. I am eternally grateful to you for simply always being there and never giving up on me.

Laura

First and foremost I would like to thank my wonderful Mum and Dad, without whose never-ending support and encouragement I would not have had the courage to take this exciting journey with Selin. Thank you also to my sister Hannah and my loyal friends, who know who they are and have all done their bit to make Oklava a reality.

I will second Selin's thank yous, in particular a big thanks to our fantastic staff. Matt, Elisa and Steph have done a wonderful job of supporting me through our exciting first year and some of the brilliant (if we do say so ourselves) drinks recipes in this book would not be there without them. Thanks to all those in the industry who have helped both guide my career and make our dream of Oklava happen, particularly all those at Salt Yard Group, where I spent five happy years prior and learnt a huge amount.

Thanks of course to Selin herself for being such a uniquely talented business partner and to her family, who welcomed us so warmly in Cyprus – particularly her grandparents and her mum Pervin, who has changed my idea of packing a suitcase well forever.

Finally a mention for my little Ollie, who I was pregnant with during our opening and when writing this book. Thank you for inspiring me to keep pushing forwards and pursuing this dream, I only hope to make you proud.